SNOWDEN

SNOWDEN
TED RALL

NEW YORK / OAKLAND

ACKNOWLEDGMENTS

Sandy Dijkstra, Jon Gilbert, Lauren Hooker, Stephanie McMillan, Bonnie D. Miller, Dan Simon, Cole Smithey, Ben Wizner

■　■　■

Seven Stories Press
140 Watts Street
New York, NY 10013
www.sevenstories.com

Library of Congress Cataloging-in-Publication Data

Rall, Ted.
Snowden / Ted Rall. -- A Seven Stories Press First Edition.
   pages cm
ISBN 978-1-60980-635-4 (paperback)
 1. Snowden, Edward J., 1983- 2. United States. National Security Agency/Central Securi
Service. 3. Leaks (Disclosure of information)--United States. 4. Whistle blowing--United
States. 5. Electronic surveillance--United States. 6. Domestic intelligence--United States
I. Title.
JF1525.W45R35 2015
327.1273--dc23

                                            2015002224

Printed in the USA.

9 8 7 6 5 4 3 2 1

SNOWDEN

SHORTLY AFTER THE END OF WORLD WAR II, GEORGE ORWELL WROTE A NOVEL IN WHICH HE IMAGINED THE WORST GOVERNMENT POSSIBLE.

IN THE NOT-DISTANT-ENOUGH FUTURE, ORWELL WARNED, A PARANOID STATE, CONSTANTLY AT WAR AND OBSESSED WITH TERRORISM, MIGHT EXPLOIT NEW TECHNOLOGY TO WATCH ITS SUBJECTS' EVERY MOVE.

NO ONE WOULD HAVE ANY PRIVACY.

THERE WOULD BE NOWHERE TO HIDE, NOWHERE TO RUN.

NOWHERE TO JUST BE YOURSELF.

EVERY COMMUNICATION -- EVERY
TELEPHONE CALL, EVERY LETTER --
WOULD BE INTERCEPTED,
ANALYZED, AND STORED IN A FILE.

THE INFORMATION IN THAT DOSSIER
COULD AND WOULD BE USED
AGAINST ANYONE THE
GOVERNMENT TARGETED, FOR ANY
REASON, AT ANY TIME.

SECURITY CAMERAS, HELICOPTERS,
AND SATELLITES WOULD TRACK
PEOPLE'S MOVEMENTS AS THEY
MOVED THROUGH THE STREETS.

GOVERNMENT SPIES WOULD WATCH THEIR SUBJECTS 24-7. EVERY HOME IN ORWELL'S FICTIONAL "OCEANIA" FEATURED A "TELESCREEN" -- A TV WITH A TWIST.

ANOTHER GLORIOUS VICTORY!

WHENEVER THEY WANTED TO WATCH THEIR SUBJECTS IN THEIR HOMES, GOVERNMENT AGENTS COULD TUNE IN.

FEW AMERICANS WOULD HAVE IMAGINED, READING 1984 DURING THE COLD WAR, THAT ORWELL'S VISION WOULD BE REALIZED -- IN THE UNITED STATES OF ALL PLACES.

ORWELL WORRIED THAT THE SOVIET MODEL WOULD EXPAND INTO GLOBAL TOTALITARIANISM-- BUT THAT SEEMS UNLIKELY TODAY IN 1980.

IF THE PEOPLE KNEW THE TRUTH

THANKS TO A YOUNG MAN NAMED EDWARD SNOWDEN, WE KNOW THAT THE U.S. GOVERNMENT SPENT HUNDREDS OF BILLIONS OF OUR TAX DOLLARS TO BUILD THE MOST SOPHISTICATED, WIDE-RANGING, AND INTRUSIVE SURVEILLANCE APPARATUS EVER CONCEIVED... TO WATCH US.

WHILE THIS EXPANDING SECURITY STATE HAS NO FUNDING PROBLEMS, THE SOCIAL SAFETY NET SUFFERS BUDGET CUTS.

EDWARD SNOWDEN WAS A
COMPUTER SPECIALIST EMPLOYED
BY THE CIA, THE NATIONAL
SECURITY AGENCY (NSA), AND,
FINALLY, THE HONOLULU OFFICE OF
AN NSA CONTRACTING FIRM, BOOZ
ALLEN HAMILTON.

AS A SYSTEMS ADMINISTRATOR
RESPONSIBLE FOR MAINTAINING AND
REPAIRING NETWORKS, SNOWDEN WAS
GIVEN BROAD PASSWORD ACCESS
TO CLASSIFIED NSA PROGRAMS AND
FILES.

THE CIA HIRED SNOWDEN IN 2005.

WHAT SNOWDEN SAW AT THE CIA ALARMED HIM. IF AMERICANS LEARNED THE TRUTH, THEY'D PROTEST.

BUT THEY DIDN'T KNOW.

WTF ?!

SNOWDEN QUESTIONED HIS
BOSSES ABOUT NSA AND CIA
SPYING AGAINST AMERICANS.
THEY JUST BRUSHED HIM OFF.
MEANWHILE, THE GOVERNMENT'S
SNOOPING WAS GROWING
MORE EXPANSIVE, PEERING INTO
MORE AND MORE OF
OUR PRIVATE LIVES.

UNLESS SOMEONE SPOKE
UP, EDWARD CONCLUDED,
AMERICAN SOCIETY WAS AT RISK OF
BECOMING A DYSTOPIAN NIGHTMARE.

THE NSA WAS OUT TO INTERCEPT AND STORE EVERY COMMUNICATION ON EARTH, THE VAST MAJORITY OF WHICH BELONGED TO LAW-ABIDING CITIZENS...INCLUDING MILLIONS OF AMERICANS. SNOWDEN SAW THE PROOF IN COUNTLESS MEMOS AND POWERPOINT PRESENTATIONS.

HE WASN'T THE ONLY ONE TO BE CONCERNED ABOUT GOVERNMENT OVERREACH AND INTRUSIVENESS. A FEW SENATORS CALLED NSA OFFICIALS TO TESTIFY UNDER OATH. BUT THE NSA LIED. THEY SAID THEY NEVER SPIED ON AMERICANS.

THE SENATORS COULDN'T CALL THEM OUT ON THEIR LIES WITHOUT REVEALING CLASSIFIED SECRETS, WHICH WAS ILLEGAL.

SNOWDEN THOUGHT: SOMEONE'S GOT TO TELL THE TRUTH.

AROUND THAT TIME, HOWEVER, A YOUNG SENATOR FROM ILLINOIS PROMISED "HOPE" AND "CHANGE."

"Obama's campaign promises and election gave me faith that he would lead us toward fixing the problems he outlined in his quest for votes...

I did not vote ~~for him~~. I voted for a (third party).

But I believed in Obama's promises."

— Snowden

PROBABLY LIBERTARIAN

SNOWDEN DECIDED TO GIVE THE NEW PRESIDENT A CHANCE TO MAKE GOOD ON HIS PROMISES...

OBAMA CONTINUED WITH THE POLICIES OF HIS PREDECESSOR.

HE CLOSED THE DOOR ON INVESTIGATING SYSTEMIC VIOLATIONS OF LAW, DEEPENED AND EXPANDED SEVERAL ABUSIVE PROGRAMS, AND REFUSED TO SPEND THE POLITICAL CAPITAL TO END THE KIND OF HUMAN RIGHTS VIOLATIONS LIKE WE SEE IN GUANTÁNAMO, WHERE MEN STILL SIT WITHOUT CHARGE.

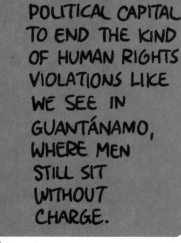

SNOWDEN SOON SAW THAT HIS FAITH HAD BEEN MISPLACED.

DISGUSTED, SNOWDEN TOOK MATTERS INTO HIS OWN HANDS.

OVER THE NEXT FEW YEARS, SNOWDEN DOWNLOADED AND SAVED A TROVE OF TOP-SECRET GOVERNMENT DOCUMENTS THAT PROVED THAT THE NSA WAS SPYING ON AMERICANS ON A VAST SCALE.

HE TOOK THIS DATA AND FLED THE UNITED STATES.

IN JUNE OF 2013, HE TURNED HIS TROVE OVER TO JOURNALISTS FOR *THE WASHINGTON POST* AND *THE GUARDIAN* NEWSPAPERS. HERE, BACKED BY IRREFUTABLE DOCUMENTARY EVIDENCE, WAS PROOF THAT THE U.S. GOVERNMENT WAS READING OUR E-MAILS AND LISTENING TO OUR PHONE CALLS.

IT WAS ONE OF THE BIGGEST LEAKS IN HISTORY. IT MADE A BIG SPLASH. EVEN SENATORS WHO HAD DEFENDED THE NSA WERE FURIOUS TO LEARN THE AGENCY HAD LIED TO THEM.

FOREIGN LEADERS, INCLUDING ALLIES, ACCUSED THE U.S. OF LISTENING TO THEIR PERSONAL PHONE CALLS.

CERTAIN SURVEILLANCE ACTIVITIES HAVE BEEN IN EFFECT FOR **MORE THAN A DECADE** AND [WE WERE] NOT SATISFACTORILY INFORMED.

THIS IS LIKE THE **STASI!**

DIRECTOR OF NATIONAL INTELLIGENCE JAMES CLAPPER'S SMUG REACTION MADE A SERIOUS CRISIS WORSE. HE RESORTED TO SEMANTIC GAMES, LIKE TESTIFYING UNDER OATH TO THE SENATE THAT STORING A PERSON'S COMMUNICATIONS WASN'T THE SAME AS "COLLECTING IT" UNTIL SOMEONE AT THE NSA ACTUALLY LOOKED AT IT.

OF THOSE BOOKS IN THAT META-PHORICAL LIBRARY, TO ME, **COLLECTION** OF U.S. PERSONS' DATA WOULD MEAN TAKING THE BOOK OFF THE SHELF AND READING IT.

SO IF I **BUY** A CD, I DON'T **HAVE** IT UNTIL I **LISTEN** TO IT?

THE SNOWDEN DOCUMENTS DEPICT A GOVERNMENT THAT INTERCEPTS AND STORES OUR COMMUNICATIONS AND HACKS INTO EVERYONE'S COMPUTER FILES -- BECAUSE IT DOESN'T DIFFERENTIATE BETWEEN CITIZENS AND POTENTIAL ENEMIES OF THE STATE.

CAN YOU **BELIEVE** THIS?

EVEN WITH ALL THIS PROOF, IT'S HARD FOR THE MIND TO PROCESS.

THE LIVES OF OTHERS, A MOVIE ABOUT EAST GERMANY'S STASI SECRET POLICE, SHOWS GOVERNMENT AGENTS LISTENING TO PEOPLE'S PHONE CALLS IN REAL TIME TO TRY TO DETERMINE WHETHER THEY'RE SUBVERSIVE "ENEMIES OF THE STATE."

THE NSA WORKS DIFFERENTLY. THEIR SYSTEM IS AUTOMATED, A PRODUCT OF THE 21st-CENTURY "BIG DATA" MODEL USED BY SILICON VALLEY COMPANIES LIKE FACEBOOK. THE NSA'S GOAL IS TO GATHER EVERY FACT, EVERY COMMUNICATION, ABOUT EVERYBODY ON EARTH.

Keyword Search:

bin Laden

Dates:

8 / 22 / 14 to 9 / 2 / 14

AUTOMATED KEYWORD SEARCHES LOOK FOR POTENTIALLY SUSPICIOUS WORDS LIKE "TERRORISM" OR "BOMB," OR "REVOLUTION."

ANALYSTS COMB THE RESULTS TO DECIDE WHETHER THE FLAGGED ITEMS CALL FOR FURTHER INVESTIGATION.

WHEREVER YOU PICK UP THE PHONE, AS SOON AS YOU START TALKING, VOICE RECOGNITION SOFTWARE TELLS THE AGENCY WHERE YOU ARE..

THE DOCUMENTS SNOWDEN TOOK, FOR EXAMPLE, SHOW THAT THE NSA INTERCEPTS AND STORES 99% OF THE "METADATA" OF AMERICANS' PHONE CALLS.

METADATA = NUMBER CALLED FROM, NUMBER CALLED TO, DURATION OF CALL, LOCATION OF CALLER, AND RECIPIENT.

A PROGRAM CALLED "MYSTIC" RECORDS 100% OF THE AUDIO CONTENT OF PHONE CALLS IN SOME COUNTRIES. SOME SAY IT CAPTURES 80% OF U.S. CALLS AS WELL.

REMEMBER THAT CALL YOU MADE ON FEB. 4, 2012, AT 11:02? THE NSA DOES.

SYMBOLIC REPRESENTATION OF
NSA DATA FARM
BLUFFDALE, UTAH

LOTS O' SERVERS

ANOTHER PROGRAM, "RETRO," ALLOWS THE NSA TO PLAY BACK CALLS AS OLD AS FIVE YEARS.

NSA PROGRAMS CALLED "BLARNEY,"
"FAIRVIEW," "OAKSTAR," "LITHIUM,"
AND "STORMBREW" CAN INTERCEPT
AND STORE 75% OF ALL INTERNET
TRAFFIC IN THE U.S.: E-MAIL, TEXT
MESSAGES, WEB BROWSING, APP
ACTIVITY, VOICE OVER INTERNET
PHONE CALLS, ONLINE BANKING,
VIDEO.

THESE PROGRAMS MARKED A RADICAL DEPARTURE FROM THE TRADITIONAL BALANCE BETWEEN SECURITY AND PRIVACY.

BEFORE 9/11, INTELLIGENCE AND LAW ENFORCEMENT AGENCIES WHO WANTED TO SPY ON AN AMERICAN CITIZEN HAD TO CONVINCE A JUDGE THAT THERE WAS SUFFICIENT "PROBABLE CAUSE" OF ILLEGAL ACTIVITY TO JUSTIFY ISSUING A WARRANT AUTHORIZING THE PROPOSED SURVEILLANCE.

RATHER THAN WAIT FOR A CRIMINAL
TO ACT OR ACCIDENTALLY MAKE
HIS PLANS KNOWN, THE NSA
PREFERED TO IDENTIFY HIM BEFORE-
HAND -- BY LISTENING TO HIS PHONE
CALLS, READING HIS E-MAILS, ETC.

THE PROBLEM WAS, THERE WERE
BILLIONS OF CALLS AND E-MAILS.

HOW COULD THEY FIND THEIR
"NEEDLE" -- SAY, A TERRORIST --

IN THE "HAYSTACK" OF DIGITAL
DATA?

THE NSA'S SOLUTION WAS TO COLLECT THE HAYSTACK.

THEY "HOOVERED" UP EVERY BIT AND BYTE OF DATA THEY COULD. THEY STORED IT IN A VAST DIGITAL "LIBRARY" OF SERVERS.

THAT WAY, NSA ANALYSTS COULD SEARCH THE HAYSTACK -- REALLY, A WHOLE BUNCH OF HAYSTACKS -- AT THEIR LEISURE.

UNDER ITS CHARTER, HOWEVER, THE NSA IS AUTHORIZED ONLY TO COLLECT "SIGNALS INTELLIGENCE" -- SPYING ON COMMUNICATIONS -- ABOUT PEOPLE OVERSEAS.

SCREENSHOT FROM THE NSA.GOV WEBSITE:

NATIONAL SECURITY AGENCY / CENTRAL SECURITY SERVICE
Defending Our Nation. Securing The Future.

Home > About NSA > Mission

Mission

The Information Assurance mission confronts the formidable challenge of preventing foreign adversaries from gaining access to sensitive or classified national security information. The Signals Intelligence mission collects, processes, and disseminates intelligence information from foreign signals for intelligence and counterintelligence purposes and to support military operations. This Agency also enables Network Warfare operations to defeat terrorists and their organizations at home and abroad, consistent with U.S. laws and the protection of privacy and civil liberties.

(I HIGHLIGHTED THE IMPORTANT PART)

SO INTERCEPTION OF DOMESTIC CALLS IS OUTSIDE THE NSA MANDATE AND ARGUABLY ILLEGAL.

NSA OFFICIALS DEFENDED
THEMSELVES BY POINTING OUT
THAT THEY *ARE* AUTHORIZED TO
LISTEN IN ON CALLS BETWEEN U.S.
CITIZENS AND PEOPLE OVERSEAS.

Sworn Testimony to Congress
March 12, 2013

SENATOR RON WYDEN
(DEMOCRAT OF OREGON):
" Does the NSA collect
any type of data at
all on millions or
hundreds of millions
of Americans?"

DIRECTOR OF
NATIONAL
INTELLIGENCE
JAMES CLAPPER:
"No sir... not
wittingly."

BUT ABOUT HALF OF
COMMUNICATIONS INTERCEPTED ARE
BETWEEN AMERICANS WHO AREN'T
BEING TARGETED AND GET SWEPT UP
IN THE DRAGNET ANYWAY.

IN 1984, THE TELESCREEN COULD NEVER BE TURNED OFF. THE NSA BROUGHT THAT DYSTOPIA TO LIFE.

THE AGENCY CAN USE YOUR SMARTPHONE TO TRACK YOUR MOVEMENTS AND LISTEN TO CONVERSATIONS IN YOUR HOME, EVEN IF YOUR PHONE IS POWERED DOWN TO "OFF."

PROGRAM NAME: "CAPTIVATED AUDIENCE."

SPEAKING OF THE TELESCREEN,
WHENEVER GOVERNMENT SPOOKS
WANT A PICTURE OF YOU, THE NSA
ACTIVATES YOUR LAPTOP CAMERA.

PROGRAM NAME:
"GUMFISH."

ACCORDING TO SNOWDEN, NSA
EMPLOYEES SHARE AND COMMENT
ABOUT IMAGES OF TARGETED
AMERICANS NUDE OR HAVING SEX.

THERE'S NO END TO THE NSA'S
INGENUITY. SMART TVs, THE NEW
GENERATION OF TELEVISIONS WIRED
TO THE INTERNET TO ALLOW
STREAMING AND WEB SURFING, HAVE
CAMERAS THAT THE NSA CAN USE
TO TURN THEM INTO A TELESCREEN
AS WELL, WATCHING AND
RECORDING YOUR EVERY MOVE.

THE NSA ACCESSES OUR COMMUNICATIONS THROUGH "BACK DOORS" PROVIDED BY THE BIG INTERNET AND TELECOMMUNICATIONS COMPANIES, INCLUDING GOOGLE, YAHOO, DROPBOX, AT&T, AND VERIZON.

IN 2006, RETIRED AT&T TECHIE MARK KLEIN TOLD *WIRED* MAGAZINE THAT HIS FORMER EMPLOYER WAS "COLLECTING EVERYTHING ON EVERYBODY" IN A SECRET ROOM IN ITS SAN FRANCISCO OFFICE AND FORWARDING IT TO THE NSA. IT TURNED OUT THAT MANY OTHER COMPANIES GAVE THEIR CUSTOMERS' INFORMATION TO THE NSA.

WE KNOW THESE THINGS BECAUSE EDWARD SNOWDEN TOLD US.

THE NSA HAS BUILT AN INFRASTRUCTURE THAT ALLOWS IT TO INTERCEPT **ALMOST EVERYTHING**. WITH THIS CAPABILITY, THE VAST MAJORITY OF HUMAN COMMUNICATIONS ARE AUTOMATICALLY INGESTED **WITHOUT TARGETING**.

THE SNOWDEN REVELATIONS LED TO AN AVALANCHE OF STORIES ABOUT THE EXPANSION OF THE AMERICAN SURVEILLANCE STATE. FOR EXAMPLE, AUTOMATED LICENSE PLATE RECOGNITION (ALPR) SYSTEMS ARE ALL THE RAGE AMONG LOCAL POLICE DEPARTMENTS.

COPS HAVE USED HUNDREDS OF MILLIONS OF ALPR SCANS TO BUILD LINKED DATABASES THAT CREATE A PROFILE OF WHERE MOTORISTS GO EVERY DAY. ALGORITHMS CRUNCH THE DATA TO PREDICT WHERE YOU'RE GOING BEFORE YOU EVEN KNOW.

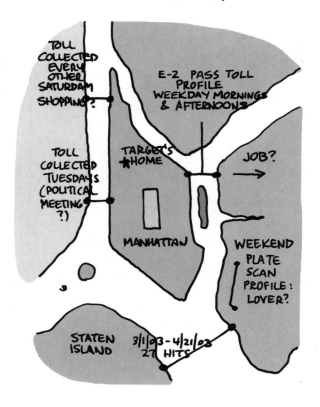

FOR MORE THAN 20 YEARS, THE
DRUG ENFORCEMENT
ADMINISTRATION (DEA) TRACKED
BILLIONS OF PHONE CALLS MADE BY
AMERICANS UNDER NO SUSPICION
OF WRONGDOING.

THE DEA CANCELED THE PROGRAM
AFTER THE NSA STORY BROKE
BECAUSE THE NSA'S EXCUSE -- THAT
THEY WERE TRACKING DANGEROUS
TERRORISTS, NOT GARDEN-VARIETY
CRIMINALS, WASN'T EVEN SLIGHTLY
TRUE.

MONEY   TECH   TRAVEL   OPINION   ☁ 78°   CROSSWORDS   YOUR TAKE   INVESTIGATIONS   VIDEO

U.S. secretly tracked billions of calls for decades

Brad Heath, **USA TODAY**   10:36 a.m. EDT April 8, 2015

THE JUSTICE DEPARTMENT STILL
REFUSES TO PUBLICLY
ACKNOWLEDGE THE DEA PROGRAM.

EVEN THE OLD-FASHIONED POST OFFICE
IS SPYING ON YOU.

THE USPS'S "MAIL-COVERS" PROGRAM IS
100 YEARS OLD. NEW SCANNING
TECHNOLOGY HAS LED TO ITS EXPANSION.
THEIR "MAIL ISOLATION CONTROL AND
TRACKING" OPERATION SCANS AND
STORES THE 160 BILLION PIECES OF MAIL
SENT BY AMERICANS EVERY YEAR.

ONE HIGH-PROFILE ABUSE OF THE "MAIL COVERS" PROGRAM TOOK PLACE IN 2011. RIGHT-WING ARIZONA SHERIFF JOE ARPAIO -- NOTORIOUS FOR PRISON CAMPS IN THE DESERT WHERE INMATES ARE FORCED TO WEAR PINK UNDERWEAR AND SOMETIMES DIE FROM THE HEAT -- USED MAIL COVER SURVEILLANCE AGAINST A POLITICAL RIVAL TO DRIVE HER OUT OF THE RESTAURANT BUSINESS.

THE COUNTY PAID $1 MILLION TO SETTLE HER LAWSUIT AGAINST ARPAIO.

HE'S STILL SHERIFF.

NOTHING WAS OFF-LIMITS TO THE NSA.

WHEN THEY LEARNED THAT SOME SMART-PHONE APPS ARE "LEAKY" -- THEY SEND PERSONAL DATA LIKE AGE, GENDER, AND EVEN SEXUAL KINKS OVER THE INTERNET -- THEY TARGETED THEM.

LIKE J. EDGAR HOOVER'S FBI, THE NSA WAS OBSESSED WITH SEX. THEY MONITORED THE PORN-SURFING HISTORIES OF MUSLIM "RADICALIZERS" WITH A VIEW TOWARD EXPLOITING THEIR "PERSONAL VULNERABILITIES" -- DISCREDITING AND UNDERMINING THEIR CREDIBILITY.

(TS//SI//REL TO USA, FVEY/FISA) The third chart includes the radicalizers' presumed areas of authority, countries of resonance, and vulnerabilities as reported and documented in 3/RA/501518-12 202017Z JUN 12, "Terrorism/Islamic Radicalization: Global Radicalizers Vulnerable in Terms of Authority."

(TS//SI//REL TO USA, FVEY/FISA)

RADICALIZERS	AUTHORITY	ARGUMENT	COUNTRIES WITH HIGHEST RESONANCE	VULNERABILITIES
name redacted	Imprisoned for inciting hatred against non-Muslims	Non-Muslims are a threat to Islam	identifying information redacted	-Online promiscuity -May misdirect donations -Desire to stay out of jail results in inconsistent arguments
name redacted	Respected academic, promotes al-Qai'da (AQ) propaganda	Offensive jihad is justified	identifying information redacted	- Online promiscuity - Publishes articles without checking facts

Golden Nugget!

Perfect Scenario – Target uploadin[g] photo to a social media site taker[s] with a mobile device.

What can we get?

54

IT'S NOT JUST AMERICANS. NOT ONLY DOES THE NSA SPY ON EVERYONE IN THE WORLD, BUT THEY ALSO GIVE THE RESULTING DATA TO THEIR SPY "PARTNERS." FOR EXAMPLE, THE GCHQ, BRITAIN'S NSA, USES NSA DATA TO DODGE LAWS THAT SUPPOSEDLY PROTECT THE PRIVACY OF BRITONS.

A DATA DRAGNET OPERATION AS HUGE AS THE NATIONAL SECURITY AGENCY REQUIRES TENS OF THOUSANDS OF EMPLOYEES AND HUNDREDS OF THOUSANDS OF OUTSOURCED SECURITY "CONTRACTORS" LIKE EDWARD SNOWDEN.

THAT'S A LOT OF PEOPLE. THEY'RE SUPPOSED TO KEEP A LOT OF SECRETS.

THEY'RE SUPPOSED TO KEEP QUIET ABOUT THINGS THAT THE REST OF US THINK ARE WRONG.

1.4 MILLION AMERICANS HAD "TOP SECURITY" CLEARANCE IN 2011. THIS GAVE THEM ACCESS TO MANY OF THE SAME DOCUMENTS AS EDWARD SNOWDEN.

*DEPARTMENT OF HOMELAND SECURITY: DEFENSE INTELLIGENCE AGENCY

WHY DIDN'T THEY SPEAK UP ABOUT THESE PROGRAMS?

WHY DID SNOWDEN?

THERE WERE MANY REASONS FOR
SNOWDEN'S PEERS TO FOLLOW
ORDERS, TO KEEP ON KEEPING ON.

MANY OF THOSE 1.4 MILLION INTELLIGENCE COMMUNITY EMPLOYEES, IT IS SAFE TO ASSUME, BOUGHT INTO PRESIDENT OBAMA'S ARGUMENT THAT THEIR SPYING PROGRAMS WERE LEGAL, NECESSARY, OR BOTH.

I CAME IN WITH A HEALTHY SKEPTICISM ABOUT THESE PROGRAMS. MY TEAM EVALUATED THEM. WE SCRUBBED THEM THOROUGHLY... MY ASSESSMENT WAS THAT THEY HELP US PREVENT TERRORIST ATTACKS.

BUT FEAR, NO DOUBT, SILENCED SPIES WHO SHARED SNOWDEN'S DOUBTS ABOUT THE LEGALITY OF PROGRAMS, LIKE "PRISM," THAT INDISCRIMINATELY SWEEP UP EVERY BIT OF DATA THEY CAN.

SO THEY KEPT SILENT.

ANOTHER REASON TO KEEP QUIET WAS A CONTRACTUAL OBLIGATION TO DO SO. EMPLOYEES OF THE NSA, CIA, FBI, AND PRIVATE SECURITY SUBCONTRACTORS, INCLUDING THE ONE FOR WHICH SNOWDEN WORKED, SIGNED EMPLOYEE CONTRACTS CONTAINING CLAUSES REQUIRING THEM NOT TO DIVULGE ANY CLASSIFIED INFORMATION.

Booz | Allen | Hamilton

EMPLOYMENT AGREEMENT

_____, 2013

Mr. Eduard Snowden
94-994 Eleu Street
Waipahu, HI 96767

Dear Mr. Snowden:
_____ pleased to offer you
_____ analyst

THERE WAS ALSO ANXIETY. AFTER 9/11, NSA OFFICIALS CLAIMED, NSA SIGNALS INTELLIGENCE PROGRAMS DISRUPTED PLOTS AND SAVED AMERICAN LIVES. IN AN AGE OF TERROR, MANY BELIEVED, LEGALITY WAS A LUXURY.

NO EVIDENCE HAS EVER BEEN PRESENTED TO SUPPORT THE NSA'S CLAIM.

OTHER NSA EMPLOYEES AGREED
WITH SNOWDEN THAT THEIR WORK
VIOLATED LAWS THAT PROTECT
AMERICANS' BASIC PRIVACY RIGHTS.
THEY WORRIED THAT INTERCEPTING
AMERICANS' COMMUNICATIONS
DISTRACTED THEM FROM THEIR JOB
OF IDENTIFYING FOREIGN
TERRORISTS.

PERHAPS MANY AGENTS WANTED
TO SPEAK UP. BUT THEY KNEW
THAT PREVIOUS WHISTLEBLOWERS'
LIVES HAD BEEN DESTROYED,
UNDERMINED, OR THREATENED.

Thomas Drake

Worked
within
the
"system"

Charged
with
espionage
&
black-
balled

NSA Whistleblower

NATURALLY, THEY WERE AFRAID.

SNOWDEN WAS WORRIED TOO. HE KNEW THAT BECOMING A WHISTLEBLOWER WAS DANGEROUS, THAT IT MIGHT LAND HIM IN PRISON, OR GET HIM KILLED.
COURAGE IS DOING THE RIGHT THING WHEN YOU'RE SCARED.

Добро пожаловать в Москву
Welcome to Moscow

BUT...

WHY?

MORE
HARM
THAN
GOOD

EDWARD JOSEPH SNOWDEN WAS BORN ON THE FIRST DAY OF THE SUMMER OF 1983. HIS PARENTS HAD GONE TO THE SAME HIGH SCHOOL. AT SOME POINT, BOTH WENT TO WORK FOR THE FEDERAL GOVERNMENT, HIS MOTHER AS A DISTRICT COURT CLERK, HIS FATHER AS A CAREER COAST GUARD OFFICER.

Born
6-21-83

Elizabeth City,
North Carolina

Lonnie Snowden   Wendy Snowden
Met: Northeastern High School
Married in 1979

IN THE EARLY 1990s, WHILE EDDIE
WAS IN ELEMENTARY SCHOOL, THE
SNOWDENS DECIDED TO MOVE TO
CROFTON, MARYLAND, TO TAKE
NEW FEDERAL JOBS. GEOGRAPHY
PROVED FATEFUL.

GENEROUS GOVERNMENT AND
NONGOVERNMENT SALARIES AND
BENEFITS IN THE INTELLIGENCE
COMMUNITY ENSURED A HIGH
QUALITY OF LIFE. CROFTON WAS
SAFE. PRETTY. CLEAN.

AT FIRST GLANCE, EDDIE SNOWDEN'S CHILDHOOD IN THE D.C. SUBURB OF CROFTON WAS UNREMARKABLE. HE WAS QUIET AND THIN. PEOPLE SAID HE WAS "NICE."

A SCOUT IS TRUSTWORTHY, BRAVE CLEAN

AND

HELPFUL COURT-EOUS

REVERENT

HE WAS AN ACTIVE MEMBER OF BOY SCOUT TROOP 731, WHICH MET AT A PRESBYTERIAN CHURCH IN CROFTON. HIS FORMER SCOUTMASTERS AND FELLOW SCOUTS SAY EDDIE DIDN'T STAND OUT.

FELLOW SCOUT JOHN BALDWIN:

MY TROOP FIT THE STEREOTYPE OF HAVING A LOT OF WEIRD LITTLE GUYS — COMPUTER NERDS WHO LOVED TO RUN AROUND IN THE WOODS. EDDIE WASN'T A TROUBLEMAKER OR ANYTHING.

JUST SHY AND FRIENDLY.

DID EDDIE INCORPORATE SCOUTING'S PHILOSOPHY OF HONESTY AND INTEGRITY FULLY INTO HIS CHARACTER? WAS HIS ADULT DISGUST AT VIOLATIONS OF THESE VALUES BY HIGH-RANKING OFFICIALS HEAVILY INFLUENCED BY THIS YOUTHFUL EMBRACE OF SCOUTING IDEALS?

ON MY HONOR
    I WILL DO MY BEST
TO DO MY DUTY TO GOD
    AND MY COUNTRY
    AND T   OBEY
    THE   LAWS
TO HELP   PEOPLE
    AT AL   IMES
    TO KE   YSELF
PHYSICA   STRONG
MEN   WAKE
                 RIGHT

IF NOTHING ELSE, HIS CAREFUL PLANNING BEFORE TURNING AGAINST THE NSA SHOWS THAT HE TOOK THE BOY SCOUT MOTTO, "BE PREPARED," TO HEART!

BRAD GUNSON ATTENDED CROFTON MIDDLE
SCHOOL AND ARUNDEL HIGH SCHOOL WITH
SNOWDEN. GUNSON REMEMBERS THAT EDDIE
HAD A HIGH VOICE, AND THAT HE HAD THE
SAME FEATHERED SHORT-BACK-AND-SIDES
BLOND HAIR AS NOW.

HE LIKED FANTASY GAMES,
VIDEO GAMES. THERE WAS
THIS WEIRD TREND WHEN
WE WERE KIDS – A
KILLING GAME I CAN'T
REMEMBER. AND MAGIC
CARDS. I REMEMBER
HIM BEING INTO THAT.

1993-

MAGIC
DECKMASTER

Magic: The Gathering

PERHAPS EDDIE'S HOMETOWN WAS AN INFLUENCE.

CROFTON IS A PLACE OF SECRETS, WHERE MANY GOVERNMENT EMPLOYEES AND PRIVATE CONTRACTORS WITH TOP-LEVEL SECURITY CLEARANCES LIVE. ADULTS DON'T TELL THEIR SPOUSES WHAT THEY DO AT WORK; SPOUSES KNOW NOT TO ASK.

TEENAGERS, SNOWDEN'S CROFTON CONTEMPORARIES RECALL, PICKED UP THE DISCREET VIBE. LIKE THEIR PARENTS, THEY TENDED TO KEEP TO THEMSELVES.

GEOGRAPHY: 25 MILES NORTH OF WASHINGTON IN FORT MEADE, MARYLAND, 30,000 NSA EMPLOYEES INTERCEPT AND PROCESS A TSUNAMI OF INFORMATION CAPTURED FROM THE WORLD'S DIGITAL, SATELLITE, AND BROADCAST COMMUNICATIONS NETWORKS.

THEY CALL IT "THE PUZZLE PALACE."

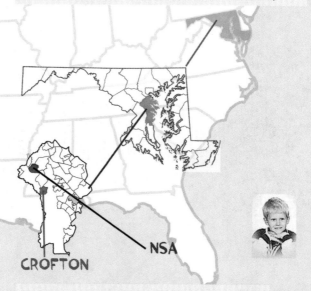

CROFTON

NSA

THE PUZZLE PALACE IS FIVE MILES DOWN THE ROAD FROM CROFTON.

THE NSA AND ITS NUMEROUS PRIVATE CORPORATE CONTRACTORS, WHICH HAVE OFFICES IN NEARBY INDUSTRIAL PARKS, DOMINATE THE COMMUNITY.

THE NSA, JOKINGLY CALLED "NO SUCH AGENCY" BECAUSE IT ISN'T LISTED IN OFFICIAL GOVERNMENT DIRECTORIES, HAS STEADILY EXPANDED ITS REACH SINCE ITS FOUNDING DURING THE 1940s. BY THE 1980s, ITS "ECHELON" SYSTEM SCOOPED UP ALMOST EVERY COMMUNICATION ON EARTH.

THIS IS GONNA BE **AWESOME**.

AFTER 9/11, A TERRIFIED CONGRESS AUTHORIZED THE NSA TO DO PRETTY MUCH WHATEVER IT WANTED IN THE NAME OF PROTECTING THE NATION.

IF YOU LIVE IN THE MARYLAND SUBURBS OF WASHINGTON, THE NSA IS EVERYWHERE. EVEN ON THE HIGHWAY, YOU CAN'T MISS THE AGENCY'S PRESENCE.

ORANGE COUNTY REGISTER REPORTER JOSHUA STEWART WAS ASSIGNED TO RESEARCH SNOWDEN, IN PART BECAUSE HE GREW UP IN THE AREA.

WE TRIED TO COME UP WITH SOMEONE [WHO KNEW SNOWDEN] WHO **DIDN'T** HAVE A SECURITY CONNECTION AND WE COULDN'T.

THIS IS WHERE A LOT OF PEOPLE ARE MAKING THE MONEY THAT GIVES THEM ALL THIS COMFORT.

"Everyone in my family has worked for the federal government in one way or another. I expected to pursue the same path."

—Edward Snowden

A CLASH BETWEEN SNOWDEN'S CONSERVATIVE AMBITIONS AND SURROUNDINGS, AND THE EMOTIONALLY WRENCHING TWISTS OF HIS TEENS AND EARLY ADULTHOOD, WAS PROBABLY INEVITABLE.

Older Sister Jessica

Lawyer & Researcher, Federal Research Center, Washington, DC

OF ALL THINGS, IT WAS A VIRUS THAT BEGAN EDWARD SNOWDEN'S TRANSFORMATION INTO THE WHISTLE-BLOWER WHO SHOOK THE WORLD.

AT AGE 15 EDDIE CONTRACTED MONONUCLEOSIS. HE MISSED MOST OF 10TH GRADE.

THE MEDIA IGNORED THIS DETAIL, SMEARING HIM AS A DROPOUT.

ACTUALLY, HE WAS BRILLIANT. BUT HE WAS DAUNTED BY THE CLASSWORK HE WOULD HAVE HAD TO MAKE UP. HE OPTED TO TAKE THE G.E.D. TEST INSTEAD.

CENTER FOR APPLIED LEA... AND TECHNOLOGY

HE ENROLLED IN ANNE ARUNDEL COMMUNITY COLLEGE, MARYLAND, AT AGE 16.

WHEN EDWARD ARRIVED AT ANNE ARUNDEL COMMUNITY COLLEGE, THE NSA'S PRESENCE LOOMED LARGE. THE SCHOOL HAD RECENTLY LAUNCHED A MAJOR IN CYBERSECURITY TRAINING, FOR STUDENTS INTERESTED IN WORKING FOR THE NSA AND THE DEFENSE DEPARTMENT.

HE DIDN'T TAKE THOSE COURSES. BUT HIS CLASSMATES DID.

THEY CALLED ME BACK FOR A **SECOND INTERVIEW**!

MEANWHILE, EDWARD'S INTEREST IN GENRE CULTURE -- GAMES, COMICS, AND COMPUTERS -- CONTINUED. AT AGE 18, IN 2001, SNOWDEN AND SOME FRIENDS BUILT THE WEBSITE RYUHANA PRESS, DEDICATED TO ANIME (JAPANESE ANIMATED COMICS).

THEY EDITED IT IN AN APARTMENT IN MILITARY HOUSING ON BASE AT FORT MEADE, MARYLAND:

HOME OF THE NSA.

VIDEO GAMES AND FANTASY-BASED CARD GAMING ARE CENTERED AROUND IDEAL WORLDS GOVERNED BY STRAIGHTFORWARD RULES. LIFE IN THESE REALITIES IS SIMPLE. YOU HAVE TO FOLLOW THE RULES. IF YOU DON'T, YOU LOSE.

CHEATING DOESN'T WORK. YOU MUST PLAY FAIR.

NOT LIKE IN POLITICS AND GOVERNMENT.

SNOWDEN'S PARENTS DIVORCED THREE YEARS AFTER HE LEFT HIGH SCHOOL. HIS DAD MOVED TO ALLENTOWN, PENNSYLVANIA, BUT EDWARD REMAINED IN ELLICOTT CITY, MARYLAND -- 15 MILES FROM THE NSA -- WITH HIS MOM. THEY MOVED INTO A SMALL CONDO.

THIS DOESN'T CHANGE HOW WE FEEL ABOUT YOU.

WE'LL **BOTH** ALWAYS LOVE **YOU**.

DIVORCE IS ALWAYS TRAUMATIC...

SNOWDEN HASN'T TALKED PUBLICLY ABOUT HIS PARENTS' DIVORCE. BUT MANY KIDS ARE UPSET WHEN THEIR PARENTS GET DIVORCED.

SOME ARE DEEPLY SHAKEN AFTER SEEING THAT SECURITY CAN BE AN ILLUSION, THAT A SACRED PROMISE CAN BE BROKEN. A PHONY SET-UP. THESE KIDS SOMETIMES FEEL THAT THEIR CHILDHOODS HAVE BEEN NOTHING BUT A BIG LIE.

NO ONE, THEY MAY DECIDE, CAN TRULY BE TRUSTED.

87

THROUGHOUT THE TUMULT OF
SNOWDEN'S TEEN YEARS AND
EARLY ADULTHOOD, HOWEVER,
THERE WAS ONE CONSTANT: HIS
INTEREST IN TECHNOLOGY. GAMING,
PROGRAMMING, SOCIAL MEDIA,
CHATTING ONLINE.

THE INTERNET, HE POSTED TO A
DISCUSSION FORUM, WAS "THE
MOST IMPORTANT INVENTION IN
ALL HUMAN HISTORY."

CLUES TO HIS LIFE AND HOW HIS OUTLOOK
EVOLVED MAY BE FOUND IN THE
DISCUSSION FORUMS AT THE TECH NEWS
SITE *ARS TECHNICA*. ANONYMOUS POSTS
UNDER THE USER NAME "THE TRUE HOOHA"
BEGAN TO APPEAR IN 2001, WHEN SNOWDEN
WAS 17. IGNORING THE 9/11 ATTACKS, THEY
COVERED SEX, CAREERS, AND GAMING.
SNOWDEN HAS NEITHER CONFIRMED NOR
DENIED THAT HE WAS "THE TRUE HOOHA."

BY 2003 HE
WAS
ALREADY
INTERESTED IN
ANONYMITY:

IS IT POSSIBLE TO
REROUTE -ALL-
TRAFFIC THROUGH A
REMOTE PROXY? BY
ALL, I MEAN TRAFFIC
SUCH AS SMTP AS
OPPOSED TO THE
STANDARD HTTP/FTP/
SSH/SOCKS.

BY THE TIME THE POSTS END IN 2012, SNOWDEN WAS 28, A FULLY REALIZED ADULT.

IRONICALLY, SOME OF "THE TRUE HOOHA" POSTS CONDEMN WHISTLEBLOWERS.

```
< TheTrueHOOHA> HOLY SHIT
                http://www.nytimes.com/2009/01/11/washington/11iran.html?_r=1&hp

< TheTrueHOOHA> WTF NYTIMES

< TheTrueHOOHA> Are they TRYING to start a war?
                Jesus christ
                they're like wikileaks

      < User19> they're just reporting, dude.

< TheTrueHOOHA> They're reporting classified shit

      < User19> shrugs

< TheTrueHOOHA> about an unpopular country surrounded by enemies already engaged
                in a war
                and about our interactions with said country regarding planning
                sovereignity violations of another country
                you don't put that shit in the NEWSPAPER

      < User19> meh

< TheTrueHOOHA> moreover, who the fuck are the anonymous sources telling them
                this?

< TheTrueHOOHA> those people should be shot in the balls.

< TheTrueHOOHA> But the tense exchanges also prompted the White House to step up
                intelligence-sharing with Israel and brief Israeli officials on
                new American efforts to subtly sabotage Iran's nuclear
                infrastructure, a major covert program that Mr. Bush is about to
                hand off to President-elect Barack Obama.

< TheTrueHOOHA> HELLO? HOW COVERT IS IT NOW? THANK YOU

      < User19> meh

< TheTrueHOOHA> I wonder how many hundreds of millions of dollars they just
                completely blew.

      < User19> you're over reacting. its fine.

< TheTrueHOOHA> It's not an overreaction. They have a HISTORY of this shit

      < User19> with flowersand cake.

      < User20> [User21]'s mushrooms are :o

< TheTrueHOOHA> these are the same people who blew the whole "we could listen to
                osama's cell phone" thingthe same people who screwed us on
                wiretappingover and over and over againThank god they're going
                out of business.

      < User19> the NYT?

< TheTrueHOOHA> Hopefully they'll finally go bankrupt this year.
                yeah.
```

LIKE MANY MILLENNIALS, HE LIKED
JAPANESE MANGA (COMICS) AND
VIDEO GAMES LIKE THE FIGHTING
GAME *TEKKEN*. *TEKKEN*, HE'D SAY
LATER, INFLUENCED
HIS SENSE OF
RIGHT AND WRONG.

HE TOLD HIS
CORRESPONDENTS
HE WAS
ATTRACTED TO
ASIAN WOMEN.

IN MARCH 2003, PRESIDENT GEORGE W. BUSH ORDERED U.S. FORCES TO INVADE IRAQ. UNEMPLOYED AND FEELING AIMLESS, SNOWDEN ENLISTED IN THE U.S. ARMY (INSTEAD OF THE COAST GUARD, AS HIS FATHER HAD).

HE WAS DETERMINED TO GET ADMITTED TO THE ELITE SPECIAL FORCES.

AT THIS POINT SNOWDEN'S POLITICS WERE IMMATURE AND CONFLICTED, SPLIT BETWEEN RIGHT-OF-CENTER PATRIOTISM/ NATIONALISM AND A NAÏVE/YOUTHFUL DESIRE TO HELP IRAQIS UNDER THE YOKE OF SADDAM'S DICTATORSHIP.

" I wanted to fight in the Iraq War

because I felt like I had an obligation as a human being...

"... to help free people from oppression."

IT WAS A FIASCO. SHORTSIGHTED AND HOBBLED BY HIS "NARROW FEET," HE WASHED OUT OF TRAINING AT FORT BENNING, GEORGIA DURING SUMMER 2004.

IN THE END, THE ARMY DIS- CHARGED HIM AFTER HE BROKE BOTH HIS FEET IN A TRAINING ACCIDENT.

FOR SNOWDEN, MILITARY SERVICE WASN'T MEANT TO BE.

GIVEN HIS IMMEDIATE DISTASTE FOR
HIS WOULD-HAVE-BEEN FELLOW
WARRIORS, IT WAS PROBABLY FOR
THE BEST.

THE SCALES
BEGAN TO
FALL
FROM
HIS
EYES. AMERICA
WAS REVEALING
ITSELF.

MOST OF THE
PEOPLE TRAIN-
ING US SEEMED
PUMPED UP
ABOUT KILLING
ARABS, NOT
HELPING
ANYONE.

OUT OF THE ARMY WITHOUT A JOB, SNOWDEN FOLLOWED THE PATH OF LEAST RESISTANCE, SEARCHING FOR EMPLOYMENT WITH THE BIGGEST LOCAL EMPLOYER.

IN 2005, HE LANDED AT THE NSA.

WHEN SNOWDEN'S STORY BROKE,
MEDIA REPORTS ABOUT HIS
BACKGROUND INCLUDED
INCREDULOUS ACCOUNTS OF THE
WUNDERKIND WHO BEGAN AT THE NSA
AS A SECURITY GUARD AND WHOSE
TALENTS WERE NOTICED, *GOOD WILL
HUNTING*-LIKE, SETTING HIM ON THE
COURSE TO A SIX-FIGURE SALARY
BEFORE AGE 30.

IT WAS TRUE.

BUT YOU PROBABLY WON'T BE
SURPRISED TO LEARN THAT IT WAS
MORE COMPLICATED THAN THAT.

HE DID INDEED BEGIN AS A SECURITY GUARD. BUT HE SOON SCORED A TECH GIG, PROBABLY THANKS TO HIS MILITARY SERVICE. HIS NEW EMPLOYER WAS THE CENTER FOR ADVANCED STUDY OF LANGUAGE, AN NSA FRONT AT THE UNIVERSITY OF MARYLAND THAT STUDIES BEHAVIORAL PSYCHOLOGY.

CASL WAS AN NSA BACKWATER, BUT ITS PROXIMITY TO FORT MEADE GAVE IT CLOSE TIES TO THE INTELLIGENCE COMMUNITY.

SNOWDEN STAYED AT CASL FOR LESS THAN A YEAR. BY LATE 2005 HIS SCHMOOZING AND TECHNICAL EXPERTISE SCORED HIM A JOB AT THE CIA. "I HAVE NO DEGREE, NOT EVEN A HIGH SCHOOL DIPLOMA," HE POSTED. "I'M CLAIMING ONLY SIX YEARS OF EXPERIENCE. IT'S TOUGH TO 'BREAK IN,' BUT ONCE YOU LAND A 'REAL' POSITION, YOU'RE MADE."

IN 2007, WHEN SNOWDEN WAS 24, THE CIA TRANSFERRED HIM OVERSEAS UNDER STATE DEPARTMENT COVER. AS A "TELECOMMUNICATIONS INFORMATION SYSTEMS OFFICER," HE RAN CYBERSECURITY FOR U.S. DIPLOMATS STATIONED AT THE U.S. PERMANENT MISSION IN GENEVA.

PREVIOUSLY SNOWDEN'S WORLDVIEW
HAD BEEN PAROCHIAL. HE BELIEVED IN
AMERICAN "EXCEPTIONALISM." HIS
EUROPEAN ASSIGNMENT, WHICH BEGAN
IN 2007, BROADENED HIS HORIZONS
BY INTRODUCING HIM TO NEW PEOPLE
WITH OTHER IDEAS.

MEANWHILE, WHAT HE SAW ON THE
JOB IN SWITZERLAND MADE HIM
QUESTION WHETHER HE WAS REALLY
WORKING ON THE SIDE OF THE
ANGELS.

IN EUROPE, SNOWDEN FOUND HIMSELF IN A PLACE WHERE THE 50-YARD LINE OF POLITICS IS FARTHER TO THE LEFT THAN BACK IN THE STATES.

LIKE ALL EUROPEANS, THE SWISS LOVE TO DISCUSS POLITICS.

NOT ONLY WAS HE EXPOSED TO DIFFERENT POINTS OF VIEW, BUT HE ALSO MET PEOPLE WITH OTHER VALUE SYSTEMS.

SNOWDEN'S WORLD GOT A LOT BIGGER.

NOT ONLY WAS HE A COG IN THE MACHINERY OF THE WORLD'S MOST DOMINANT COUNTRY...

HIS SENSE OF PERSONAL RESPONSIBILITY WAS GROWING.

LATE-NIGHT BULL SESSIONS WEREN'T THE BIGGEST FACTOR IN HIS POLITICAL EVOLUTION.

HIS LONG-HELD FAITH IN THE AMERICAN SYSTEM AND HIS LIBERTARIAN BELIEFS THAT THE GOVERNMENT THAT GOVERNS BEST GOVERNS LEAST WERE TESTED BY THE ELECTION OF PRESIDENT BARACK OBAMA.

SNOWDEN DIDN'T VOTE FOR OBAMA. LIKE MANY DEMOCRATS, HOWEVER, HE WAS DISAPPOINTED BY THE NEW PRESIDENT'S EMBRACE OF REALPOLITIK OVER IDEALISM.

OBAMA DECIDED TO LET THOSE RESPONSIBLE FOR HUMAN RIGHTS ABUSES UNDER GEORGE W. BUSH OFF SCOT-FREE. AND HE WAS POLITICIZING NATIONAL INTELLIGENCE:

"Obama just appointed a fucking POLITICIAN to run the CIA! I'm so angry right now."

A 2008 INCIDENT MADE HIM SERIOUSLY RECONSIDER THE CIA AND AMERICA'S ROLE IN THE WORLD.

GENEVA-BASED AGENTS HAD BLACKMAILED A SWISS BANKER BY GETTING HIM DRUNK, ENCOURAGING HIM TO DRIVE HOME, THEN HAVING THE LOCAL POLICE ARREST HIM. NATURALLY, THE CIA GOT HIM OUT OF LEGAL TROUBLE, BUT AT A PRICE: SECRET FINANCIAL DATA SOUGHT BY THE CIA.

MEANWHILE, INTELLIGENCE AGENTS TOLD HIM THE WAR AGAINST IRAQ AND U.S. FOREIGN POLICY IN THE MIDDLE EAST WERE COUNTER-PRODUCTIVE. "THE CIA CASE OFFICERS WERE ALL GOING, 'WHAT THE HELL ARE WE DOING?'"

MOREOVER, THE HUMAN RIGHTS ABUSES WERE TOO OUTRAGEOUS FOR A THOUGHTFUL YOUNG MAN LIKE SNOWDEN TO IGNORE.

"THIS WAS THE BUSH PERIOD, WHEN THE WAR ON TERROR HAD GOTTEN REALLY DARK. WE WERE TORTURING PEOPLE; WE HAD WARRANTLESS WIRETAPPING," SNOWDEN WOULD SAY LATER.

"MUCH OF WHAT I SAW IN GENEVA REALLY DISILLUSIONED ME ABOUT HOW MY GOVERNMENT FUNCTIONS AND WHAT ITS IMPACT IS IN THE WORLD. I REALIZED THAT I WAS PART OF SOMETHING THAT WAS DOING FAR MORE HARM THAN GOOD."

IN 2008 AND 2009, SNOWDEN NOTICED A VULNERABILTY IN THE AGENCY'S PERSONNEL SOFTWARE. TO PROVE HIS POINT -- WITH HIS SUPERVISOR'S APPROVAL -- HE HACKED INTO IT HIMSELF.

BUT CIA EMPLOYEES HIGHER UP THE FOOD CHAIN, WHO'D PRESUMABLY SIGNED OFF ON THE SOFTWARE AND WERE PERHAPS AFRAID OF BEING EMBARRASSED, WERE SO ANGRY THAT THEY ADDED A DEROGATORY COMMENT TO SNOWDEN'S FILE.

SNOWDEN HAD ALWAYS BEEN UNHAPPY THAT THE CIA LIKED TO PUSH PETTY BUREAUCRATS UPWARDS IN THE POWER STRUCTURE.

was forced to reprimand Edward to remind him of importance of command structure, operational secur

WORKING WITHIN THE SYSTEM, HE SAW, WOULD GET YOU INTO TROUBLE. BUT THE SYSTEM WOULDN'T CHANGE.

YOU HAVE TO REPORT WRONGDOING TO THOSE MOST RESPONSIBLE FOR IT. THE SYSTEM DOES NOT WORK.

IN FEBRUARY 2009 HE RESIGNED FROM THE CIA AND JOINED THE NSA AT A FIELD OFFICE FINANCED BY DELL COMPUTER COMPANY, AT YOKOTA AIR BASE NEAR TOKYO. HIS ASSIGNMENT WAS TO ADVISE JAPANESE AND U.S. MILITARY OFFICIALS ON HOW TO PROTECT THEIR SYSTEMS FROM CHINESE HACKER ATTACKS.

THE NEW JOB CAME WITH MORE RESPONSIBILITIES AND A HIGHER SECURITY CLEARANCE. THE THINGS HE SAW INCREASED HIS DISILLUSIONMENT.

WHENEVER HE WANTED, HE COULD WATCH ON HIS SCREEN AS CIA PREDATOR DRONES BLEW UP PEOPLE IN THE MIDDLE EAST AND SOUTH ASIA.

HE READ ABOUT TARGETED KILLINGS AND ASSASSINATIONS, AND HE BECAME APPALLED BY THE INCREDIBLE REACH OF NSA SURVEILLANCE, SUCH AS THE AGENCY'S ABILITY TO TRACK EVERYONE IN A CITY THROUGH THEIR SMARTPHONES AND OTHER ELECTRONIC DEVICES.

THIS WAS NOT WHAT HE HAD
EXPECTED FROM OBAMA.

"I WATCHED AS OBAMA
ADVANCED THE VERY POLICIES
THAT I THOUGHT WOULD BE
REINED IN. I GOT HARDENED."

WHAT EDWARD SNOWDEN SAW IN JAPAN BETWEEN 2009 AND 2012 WAS A GOVERNMENT BREAKING PRIVACY RIGHTS OF AMERICANS AND PEOPLE AROUND THE WORLD WILLY-NILLY.

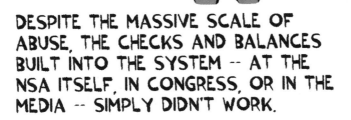

THEY ARE INTENT ON MAKING EVERY CONVERSATION AND EVERY FORM OF BEHAVIOR IN THE WORLD KNOWN TO THEM.

I HAVE BEEN LOOKING FOR LEADERS, BUT I REALIZED THAT LEADERSHIP WAS ABOUT BEING THE FIRST TO ACT.

DESPITE THE MASSIVE SCALE OF ABUSE, THE CHECKS AND BALANCES BUILT INTO THE SYSTEM -- AT THE NSA ITSELF, IN CONGRESS, OR IN THE MEDIA -- SIMPLY DIDN'T WORK.

"JAPAN MARKS A TURNING POINT," LUKE HARDING WROTE IN *THE SNOWDEN FILES*. "IT IS THE PERIOD WHEN SNOWDEN GOES FROM DISILLUSIONED TECHNICIAN TO PROTO-WHISTLEBLOWER."

IN MARCH 2012, EDWARD SNOWDEN APPLIED FOR A TRANSFER TO A GIG, OFFICIALLY AS A DELL CONTRACTOR, BUT ACTUALLY FOR THE NSA'S REGIONAL CRYPTOLOGY OFFICE NEAR HONOLULU, HAWAII.

THE "CENTRAL SECURITY SERVICE" SPECIALIZES IN SURVEILLANCE OF CHINA.

THE NSA'S LIES RELIED ON ABSENCE OF DOCUMENTARY EVIDENCE. SO HE DECIDED TO GATHER TOP-SECRET NSA FILES ABOUT THE AGENCY'S ILLEGAL SURVEILLANCE OF THE AMERICAN PEOPLE, THEN LEAK THEM TO A REPUTABLE INDEPENDENT JOURNALIST BRAVE ENOUGH TO PRESENT THE FACTS TO THE PUBLIC.

SNOWDEN KNEW THE RISKS.
THEORETICALLY, WHISTLEBLOWERS
ARE HEROES PROTECTED BY
FEDERAL LAWS.

IN REALITY, THE GOVERNMENT
TRIES TO DESTROY THEM. AFTER
DANIEL ELLSBERG LEAKED THE
PENTAGON PAPERS, NIXON
ADMINISTRATION BURGLARS BROKE
INTO HIS PSYCHIATRIST'S OFFICE
AND TOLD THE MEDIA HE WAS
CRAZY.

SNOWDEN WAS NO LONGER BLINDED BY THE NATURE OF THE U.S. INTELLIGENCE APPARATUS. ONCE HE WENT PUBLIC, HE KNEW, THE GOVERNMENT WOULD DECLARE WAR AGAINST HIM. HIS PERSONAL LIFE, CLOTHES -- EVERYTHING -- WOULD GET DISSECTED, SPUN, AND SLANDERED.

IS HE **GAY**? HE **LOOKS** GAY.

"a grandiose narcissist"

"a narcissistic young man who has decided he is smarter than the rest of us"

HE HAS A GIRL FRIEND! A **HOT** POLE DANCER! WHAT'S WITH **THAT**?

SNOWDEN HAD FOLLOWED THE CASE OF U.S. ARMY PRIVATE BRADLEY (NOW CHELSEA) MANNING, WHO'D LEAKED MILLIONS OF PAGES OF WAR LOGS ABOUT THE INVASIONS OF IRAQ AND AFGHANISTAN TO WIKILEAKS.

IT WAS A NOBLE AND COURAGEOUS ACT, BUT LARGELY WITHOUT EFFECT.

WIKILEAKS IS A WEBSITE DESIGNED TO ALLOW PEOPLE TO LEAK DOCUMENTS WHILE REMAINING ANONYMOUS. MOVING SECRETS INTO THE PUBLIC SPACE, THE THINKING GOES, ENSURES THAT DASTARDLY DEEDS WILL GET PUNISHED AFTER A VIBRANT DEBATE. BUT EVEN VIDEOS OF BRUTAL MASSACRES BY U.S. TROOPS IN IRAQ WEREN'T ENOUGH TO GET PEOPLE'S ATTENTION.

THE PUBLIC SCARCELY NOTICED THE
GRISLY FOOTAGE OF TROOPS
GLEEFULLY BLOWING AWAY IRAQI
CIVILIANS. BRADLEY WAS TORTURED
IN AN ARMY BRIG. THEY BEAT HIM
AND SUBJECTED HIM TO FORCED
NUDITY, LIKE AT THE NOTORIOUS
ABU GHRAIB PRISON IN IRAQ.

MANNING WAS COURT-MARTIALED,
SENTENCED TO 35 YEARS IN PRISON,
AND "DISAPPEARED." THERE WAS NO
MERCY. THE LESSON: DON'T LET
THEM ARREST YOU.

PERHAPS THE MOST RELEVANT
PRECEDENT FROM SNOWDEN'S POINT
OF VIEW WAS THOMAS DRAKE.
DRAKE HAD GONE THROUGH OFFICIAL
CHANNELS TO COMPLAIN ABOUT
CONFLICTS OF INTEREST AND WASTE
OF FEDERAL FUNDS AFTER 9/11.

HE WAS REPEATEDLY STONEWALLED
AND PUNISHED.

THE BUSH ADMINISTRATION HARASSED DRAKE. THEN "HOPE AND CHANGE" OBAMA PROSECUTED HIM FOR ESPIONAGE. THE GOVERNMENT CASE ULTIMATELY COLLAPSED, BUT DRAKE'S CAREER WAS IN SHAMBLES, HIS SAVINGS DRAINED, HIS MARRIAGE RUINED.

UNABLE TO FIND WORK IN THE TECH INDUSTRY, DRAKE -- A FORMER TOP NSA EXECUTIVE-- NOW WORKS AT AN APPLE STORE.

I WAS CURIOUS ABOUT THE MINDSET OF A PERSON LIKE EDWARD SNOWDEN. DOES HE HAVE A BIT OF A MARTYR COMPLEX? OR IS HE, AS SOME CRITICS HAVE ACCUSED HIM OF BEING, A SMUG KNOW-IT-ALL WITH DELUSIONS OF SUPERIORITY? TO TRY TO GAIN SOME INSIGHT, I MET WITH THOMAS DRAKE.

SNOWDEN'S LEVEL OF ACCESS WAS QUITE UN-RESTRICTED. HE WAS AN ELITE AMONG ELITES.

HE HELPED TRAIN PEOPLE TO **HACK NETWORKS**. TO TEST THE NET, YOU HAVE TO HAVE A LOT OF PRIVILEGES. I LIVED IN THAT SPACE.

DRAKE BECAME CONVINCED THAT A
POST-9/11 NSA PROGRAM CALLED
"TRAILBLAZER" WAS SWEEPING UP TOO
MANY PERSONAL COMMUNICATIONS
BETWEEN ORDINARY AMERICANS, THUS
VIOLATING THE FOURTH AMENDMENT'S
PROHIBITION AGAINST UNREASONABLE
SEARCH AND SEIZURE.

I COULDN'T STAND BY
AND WATCH IT HAPPEN.

MOREOVER, IT WAS A TREMENDOUS
WASTE OF MONEY -- THE NSA HAD
ANOTHER PROGRAM CALLED
"THINTHREAD" THAT COULD DO A
BETTER JOB, FOR A FRACTION OF THE
COST, WITHOUT THE PRIVACY
VIOLATIONS.

DRAKE'S BOSSES HAD AN INTEREST IN TRAILBLAZER'S BIG BUDGET AND TIES TO THE CONTRACTORS BEHIND IT: THEY BLEW HIM OFF. DRAKE COMPLAINED TO THE NSA'S INSPECTOR GENERAL. HE TESTIFIED TO HOUSE AND SENATE COMMITTEES IN CHARGE OF OVERSIGHT. NOTHING HAPPENED. AFTER HE WENT TO *THE BALTIMORE SUN*, SOMETHING *DID* HAPPEN: THE FBI RAIDED HIS HOME LIKE HE WAS A DRUG KINGPIN.

DRAKE SPENT FOUR YEARS FIGHTING THE CHARGES. IN THE END, HE AGREED TO PLEAD GUILTY TO A SINGLE MISDEMEANOR.

THEN YOU DISCOVER THAT YOUR OWN GOVERNMENT IS VIOLATING THE CONSTITUTION.

I CAN'T **STAND** SEEING INJUSTICE, WRONGDOING, PEOPLE PROFITING OFF THAT WRONG- DOING WITHOUT ANY ACCOUNT- ABILITY. I CHOSE TO EXERCISE MY **PERSONAL SOVEREIGNTY**.

I PRESSED: WHAT, IF ANYTHING, DID DRAKE THINK MADE HIM DIFFERENT FROM HIS COWORKERS, THE VAST MAJORITY OF WHOM WENT ALONG TO GET ALONG? I GOT THE FEELING THAT NO ONE HAD ASKED HIM THAT BEFORE.

"WELL, I GREW UP IN TEXAS AND VERMONT. REJECTING AUTHORITY, INDIVIDUALITY, INDEPENDENCE ARE VALUES THERE. I ATTENDED TOWN MEETINGS IN VERMONT -- DEMOCRACY IN ACTION."

IN HIGH SCHOOL DURING THE EARLY 1970s, HE WATCHED SENIORS BURN THEIR DRAFT CARDS. CIVIL DISOBEDIENCE, HE SAW, COULD BE POWERFUL AND EFFECTIVE.

IN THE LATE 1970s, DRAKE HAD WATCHED AS THE CHURCH COMMITTEE EXPOSED THE CIA'S ABUSES IN NATIONALLY TELEVISED HEARINGS.

YOU CAN IMAGINE WHAT IT FELT LIKE, FOR ME, TO DISCOVER IT WAS HAPPENING AGAIN.

IT WAS THE ABYSS...

WHAT'S AT STAKE IS THE RULE OF LAW.

135

AS SNOWDEN CONSIDERED HIS OPTIONS, HE KNEW THAT AS A DELL CONTRACTOR HE WASN'T COVERED BY WHISTLEBLOWER PROTECTION LAWS.

IN THE LATE SPRING OF 2013, HE CAME ACROSS A LONG MEMO ON "STELLAR WIND," AN NSA PROGRAM THAT COLLECTS TELEPHONE METADATA OF EVERY AMERICAN.

ALL REMAINING DOUBTS EVAPORATED.

SNOWDEN TRANSFERRED TO ANOTHER NSA CONTRACTOR POSITION. THE JOB PAID $122,000, MUCH LESS THAN HIS PREVIOUS $200,000 SALARY.

BUT HE WASN'T CONCERNED ABOUT A PAYCHECK.

AS A SYSTEMS ADMINISTRATOR, HE COULD SEE ANY TOP-SECRET NSA FILE -- AND NO ONE WOULD KNOW.

EVERY MOMENT HE GOT WITHOUT
SOMEONE WATCHING, SNOWDEN
COPIED FILES. HE FILLED UP ONE
THUMB DRIVE AFTER ANOTHER.

HE WAS LATER SEEN TRAVELING
WITH FOUR LAPTOPS -- BUT
THOSE WERE FOR MANAGING
SECURE COMMUNICATIONS. THE
NSA DOCUMENTS WERE
PROBABLY KEPT ON THE THUMB
DRIVES.

IT TOOK EDWARD SNOWDEN FOUR WEEKS TO DOWNLOAD THE FILES. WHEN HE WAS FINISHED, HE APPLIED FOR SICK LEAVE, USING AN EXCUSE THAT WOULD EXPLAIN A LONG ABSENCE.

IT WAS APRIL.

"EPILEPSY"?

YEAH. NO TELLING HOW LONG IT'LL TAKE.

DURING THE SAME PERIOD HE WAS SCOURING NSA SERVERS FOR INCRIMINATING INFORMATION, SNOWDEN CONTACTED CIVIL LIBERTIES ATTORNEY GLENN GREENWALD (A BLOGGER FOR SALON, THEN A COLUMNIST FOR *THE GUARDIAN*) AND HIS COLLABORATOR LAURA POITRAS, A DARING INDEPENDENT DOCUMENTARY FILMMAKER.

"I am a senior member of the intel community

IT TOOK MONTHS FOR THE THREE OF THEM TO SET UP THE ENCRYPTED COMMUNICATIONS NECESSARY TO AVOID THE NSA'S PRYING EYES, AND FOR SNOWDEN TO CONVINCE GREENWALD AND POITRAS THAT THEY COULD TRUST HIM. "I DON'T KNOW IF YOU'RE LEGIT, CRAZY, OR TRYING TO ENTRAP ME," SHE WROTE.

SNOWDEN

POITRAS
(Berlin)

GREENWALD
(Rio de Janeiro)

EDWARD FELT CONFIDENT THAT HE WAS DOING THE RIGHT THING. YES, HE HAD VIOLATED HIS EMPLOYMENT CONTRACT, BUT IN DOING SO HE HAD SIDED WITH THE GREATER GOOD: TRYING TO PREVENT HIS COUNTRY FROM DEVOLVING FURTHER INTO 1984 WITHOUT PUBLIC DEBATE.

BUT IT WASN'T EASY. HE DIDN'T DARE CONFIDE IN ANYONE -- A FRIEND, HIS PARENTS, NOT EVEN HIS GIRLFRIEND -- LEST THEY BE IMPLICATED IN THE CHARGES HE'D FACE.

THUMB DRIVES SAFELY STOWED, SNOWDEN LEFT HIS LITTLE HOUSE.

HE GOT INTO A TAXI AND
VANISHED.

FINALLY, ON JUNE 4, 2013, SNOWDEN'S PLAN BORE FRUIT. GREENWALD, POITRAS, AND A *GUARDIAN* REPORTER, EWEN MacASKILL, ARRIVED AT SNOWDEN'S FIRST HOME ON THE RUN FROM THE U.S. GOVERNMENT: A HOTEL ROOM IN HONG KONG. A NERVOUS BUT CONTROLLED SNOWDEN WALKED THE THREE JOURNALISTS THROUGH THE DOCUMENTS.

THE NSA'S COLLECTION OF ALL U.S. TELEPHONY METADATA WAS CHOSEN FOR THE FIRST STORY. NEXT WOULD BE THE "PRISM" DATA-VACUUMING OPERATION.

MAE

ANT P

(TS//SI//REL) MAESTRO-II is a miniaturized digital core packaged in a Multi-Chip M (MCM) to be used in implants with size constraining concentrations ...

(TS//SI//REL) M.......... .s the TAO standard implant architecture. The en? provides a robu............ able, standard digital platform resulting in a performance imp................ he obsolete HC12 microcontroller based des development Printe............ d (PCB) using packaged parts has been develope available as the st......... rm. The MAESTRO-II Multi-chip Module (MC3) co ARM7 microcontro............. lash and SDRAM memories.

ON THE RUN

THE GUARDIAN, THE NEW YORK TIMES, AND THE WASHINGTON POST PUBLISHED REPORTS ABOUT, AND EXCERPTS OF, SNOWDEN'S LEAKS, IGNITING A NATIONAL AND WORLDWIDE DEBATE ON THE EROSION OF INDIVIDUAL CITIZENS' RIGHTS AND THE GROWTH OF THE POWER OF THE MILITARY AND INTELLIGENCE-GATHERING INDUSTRIES.

PREDICTABLY, POLITICIANS AND
PUNDITS ACCUSED SNOWDEN OF
NAÏVETÉ, RECKLESSNESS, AND
TREASON.

ex-vice president
DICK CHENEY

ex-secy of state
HILLARY CLINTON

SNOWDEN WAS DEFIANT. "I HAVE NO
INTENTION OF HIDING WHO I AM,
BECAUSE I KNOW I HAVE DONE
NOTHING WRONG," HE REPLIED.

"I HAD THE AUTHORITIES TO WIRETAP **ANYONE**, FROM YOU OR YOUR ACCOUNTANT TO A FEDERAL JUDGE TO EVEN THE PRESIDENT IF I HAD A PERSONAL E-MAIL."

LIVE

NSA LEAKER EDWARD SNOWDEN

FORMER CONTRACTOR REVEALED "PRISM"

THIS SNOWDEN SITUATION IS INTOLERABLE. GET THIS KID IN CUSTODY!

YES, MR. PRESIDENT.

IF [SNOWDEN] BELIEVES THAT WHAT HE DID WAS RIGHT, THEN, LIKE EVERY AMERICAN CITIZEN, HE CAN COME HERE, APPEAR BEFORE THE COURT WITH A LAWYER, AND MAKE HIS CASE.

MANY AMERICANS AGREED WITH OBAMA THAT HE SHOULD FACE TRIAL. BUT THEY WEREN'T SEEING THE INCREASINGLY LIMITED OPTIONS FROM SNOWDEN'S PERSPECTIVE.

THE SNOWDEN REVELATIONS ARE ALL OVER THE INTERNET. LEGALLY, HOWEVER, THEY'RE STILL "CLASSIFIED." SO IF SNOWDEN WERE PUT ON TRIAL, A JURY WOULDN'T GET TO SEE THEM OR HEAR TESTIMONY ABOUT NSA SPYING AGAINST AMERICANS.

YOUR HONOR, THE PEOPLE HAVE BEFORE YOU A MOTION TO INVOKE THE "STATES SECRETS PRIVILEGE."

SIMILARLY, SNOWDEN'S DUTIES AS AN NSA AND CIA CONTRACTOR ARE ALL STILL CLASSIFIED.

A TRIAL WOULDN'T BE TELEVISED, SO HE WOULDN'T BE ABLE TO ARGUE HIS CASE TO THE AMERICAN PEOPLE. A TRIAL WOULD FOCUS ON ONE QUESTION: DID SNOWDEN BREAK THE LAW? THE VERDICT WAS A FOREGONE CONCLUSION: GUILTY.

MEANWHILE, THE REAL CRIMINALS WOULD REMAIN FREE TO CONTINUE BREAKING THE LAW.

JUSTICE, IN THE BROAD SENSE,
MATTERED TO EDWARD MORE THAN
THE LETTER OF THE LAW. YES, HE
WAS VIOLATING HIS CONTRACT. BUT
WHAT THE GOVERNMENT WAS DOING
WAS MUCH BIGGER AND MUCH WORSE.

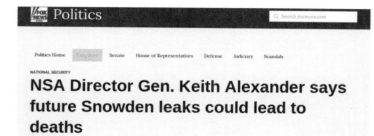

THE NSA WAS BREAKING BIG LAWS, IN
A BIG WAY, AGAINST LITERALLY
EVERYONE. *THAT* MATTERED.

NOW THE FEDS KNEW SNOWDEN WAS IN HONG KONG. HE MET WITH LAWYERS TO TRY TO FIGURE OUT WHAT TO DO AND WHERE TO GO NEXT. HE SPENT THE NEXT TWO WEEKS MOVING FROM ONE SAFEHOUSE TO ANOTHER.

Albert Ho
Snowden's
Hong Kong Lawyer

I DON'T THINK HE EVER HAD A WELL-THOUGHT-OUT PLAN. I REALLY THINK HE'S A KID.

OBAMA ADMINISTRATION OFFICIALS
WORKED THE PHONES, PRESSURING THE
CHINESE TO TURN OVER THE FUGITIVE.
THEY FORMALLY INDICTED SNOWDEN
FOR ESPIONAGE ON JUNE 21. NOW HE
FACED LIFE IN PRISON.

CRIMINAL COMPLAINT **UNDI**

I, the complainant in this case, state that the
On or about the date(s) of __May 2013__ in the county of ____
____ District of __Not Applicable__ the defendant(s

Code Section	Offense Description
18 U.S.C. 641	Theft of Government Proper
18 U.S.C. 793(d)	Unauthorized Communication of National Defense Informatio
18 U.S.C. 798(a)(3)	Willful Communication of Classi Communications Intelligence Inf to an Unauthorized Person

HOWEVER, THE CHINESE WERE
ALREADY DEALING WITH PROTESTS
OVER FREE SPEECH IN HONG KONG.
THEY DIDN'T WANT TO EXTRADITE
SNOWDEN. THEY SIGNALED THAT
THEY'D LET HIM LEAVE.

ON JUNE 22 SNOWDEN WENT TO THE HONG KONG AIRPORT. TO HIS RELIEF, THE CHINESE WERE TRUE TO THEIR WORD. HE CHECKED IN WITHOUT INCIDENT.

SNOWDEN HAD WITH HIM A REQUEST
FOR SAFE CONDUCT CERTIFICATE
ISSUED BY THE GOVERNMENT OF
ECUADOR, WHOSE EMBASSY IN
LONDON HAD GRANTED POLITICAL
ASYLUM TO WIKILEAKS FOUNDER
JULIAN ASSANGE.

HE BOARDED A FLIGHT TO
MOSCOW. FROM THERE, HE'D
CONTINUE ON TO QUITO, ECUADOR,
VIA HAVANA.

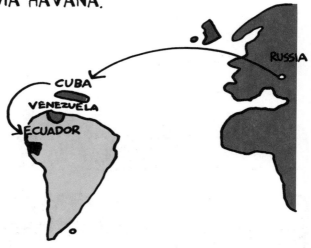

COULD HE STAY FREE? IT SEEMED
POSSIBLE.

IT WAS JUNE 23. AS HE WAS IN THE AIR, TRAVELING ALONGSIDE WIKILEAKS VOLUNTEER SARAH HARRISON, THE STATE DEPARTMENT CANCELED SNOWDEN'S PASSPORT.

IF THE U.S. HADN'T DONE THAT, HE LIKELY WOULD HAVE REACHED ECUADOR, SAFE FROM AMERICAN PROSECUTORS.

NSA CHIEF GEN. KEITH ALEXANDER

"THIS IS AN INDIVIDUAL WHO IS NOT ACTING, IN MY OPINION, WITH NOBLE INTENT."

WHILE HE WAS IN THE AIR, SPOKESMEN FOR THE AMERICAN POLITICAL ESTABLISHMENT DECLARED HIM AN ENEMY OF THE STATE. ARREST HIM! THEY DEMANDED.

"I DON'T LOOK AT THIS AS BEING A WHISTLEBLOWER. I THINK IT'S AN ACT OF TREASON."

SENATOR DIANNE FEINSTEIN

HE'S A TRAITOR. THE DISCLOSURE OF THIS INFORMATION PUTS AMERICANS AT RISK. IT SHOWS OUR ADVERSARIES WHAT OUR CAPABILITIES ARE.

HOUSE SPEAKER JOHN BOEHNER

HILLARY CLINTON

TURNING OVER A LOT OF... MATERIAL... GAVE ALL KINDS OF INFORMATION, NOT ONLY TO BIG COUNTRIES, BUT TO... TERRORIST GROUPS AND THE LIKE.

Never happened.

WHEN PEOPLE CHOOSE CIVIL DISOBEDIENCE THEY'RE AT THEIR WIT'S END... HE FELT... THIS WAS SO WRONG—MILLIONS OF PHONE RECORDS BEING LOOKED AT.

SENATOR RAND PAUL

BUT OTHERS SAW HIM AS A HERO.

AMERICANS REASONABLY EXPECT THAT THEIR MOVEMENTS, COMMUNICATIONS, AND DECISIONS WILL NOT BE RECORDED AND ANALYZED BY THE GOVERNMENT.

GEORGETOWN U. LAW PROFESSOR LAURA K. DONOHUE

MAINSTREAM POLITICIANS AND THEIR MEDIA ALLIES EMPHASIZED SNOWDEN'S FLIGHT TO HONG KONG, WHICH WAS PART OF CHINA, A U.S. RIVAL, AND THEN TO RUSSIA, WHICH WAS ENGAGED IN PROXY WARS WITH THE U.S., PLUS HIS PLANS TO CONTINUE TO VENEZUELA AND ECUADOR, BOTH GOVERNED BY SOCIALIST PRESIDENTS.

WHEN YOU LOOK AT IT, EVERY ONE OF THOSE NATIONS IS HOSTILE TO THE UNITED STATES.

IF HE COULD GO TO NORTH KOREA AND IRAN HE COULD ROUND OUT HIS... TOUR

Chairman House Intelligence Committee

MR. ROGERS

SNOWDEN'S PATRIOTISM, THEY SAID, WAS COMPROMISED BY THE FACT THAT HE WAS HOPSCOTCHING FROM ONE "ENEMY" COUNTRY TO THE NEXT, ANY ONE OF WHICH MIGHT GET THEIR HANDS ON SENSITIVE CLASSIFIED INFORMATION.

THE FIRST ARGUMENT WAS SILLY: OF *COURSE* HE FLED TO U.S. ADVERSARIES. *ALLIES* OF THE U.S. WOULD HAVE *ARRESTED* HIM. THE SECURITY CONCERN WAS VALID: BUT SNOWDEN WAS A PRO. AS FAR AS WE KNOW, NO OTHER GOVERNMENT HAS ACCESSED THE FILES.

WHAT IF THE **TERRORISTS** GOT TO ALL THAT INFO?

IF IT WAS SO VITAL, MAYBE THEY SHOULDN'T LEAVE IT WHERE ANY SYSADMIN COULD GET IT...

CLEAN UP ALL TRASH

IF ANYONE REGRETTED HIS ITINERARY, HOWEVER, IT WAS SNOWDEN HIMSELF -- AT THIS WRITING, TWO YEARS LATER, HE'S STILL STUCK IN RUSSIA. SOME BLAME RUSSIAN PRESIDENT VLADIMIR PUTIN. BUT THE PROBLEM IS LOGISTICAL: YOU CAN'T GET TO LATIN AMERICA FROM MOSCOW WITHOUT PASSING OVER THE AIR-SPACE OF U.S. ALLIES OR CLIENT STATES.

40 days @ Sheremetyevo's airport transit lounge:
SNOWDEN'S READING LIST:
Stories - Anton Chekhov
Crime and Punishment - Dostoyevsky
Complete works of Nikolai Karamzin
Russian Language 101

AS SNOWDEN COOLED HIS HEELS IN THE DIPLOMATIC LIMBO OF AN AIRPORT QUARANTINE ROOM, RUSSIAN FOREIGN MINISTER SERGEI LAVROV REFUSED TO DEPORT HIM TO THE U.S. LAVROV POINTED OUT THAT HE WAS STILL IN THE TRANSIT AREA OF THE AIRPORT, SO HE HADN'T FORMALLY ENTERED RUSSIA. ALSO, THE U.S. AND RUSSIA HAD NEVER SIGNED A BILATERAL EXTRADITION TREATY.

WE ARE IN NO WAY INVOLVED WITH MR. SNOWDEN, HIS RELATIONS WITH U.S. JUSTICE, NOR HIS MOVEMENTS AROUND THE WORLD.

RUSSIA GRANTED ASYLUM TO SNOWDEN 40 DAYS LATER.

VICE PRESIDENT JOE BIDEN HAD MORE LUCK WITH ECUADOR'S PRESIDENT, WHOM HE BULLIED AND CAJOLED INTO REVOKING THE SAFE-CONDUCT PASS.

THE LACK OF A NATION WILLING TO GRANT ASYLUM TO SNOWDEN, COUPLED WITH THE INABILITY TO AVOID TRAVEL OVER COUNTRIES FRIENDLY TO THE U.S., MEANT THAT SNOWDEN COULDN'T LEAVE RUSSIA.

HE WAS FRIENDLY AND VERY CORDIAL.

RAFAEL CORREA
PRESIDENT, ECUADOR

I'M NOT GOING TO BE SCRAMBLING JETS TO GET A 29-YEAR-OLD HACKER.

PUBLICLY, OBAMA PLAYED IT COOL. BEHIND THE SCENES, HE AND HIS STAFF WERE FREAKING OUT BECAUSE SNOWDEN HAD EMBARRASSED THEM, EXPOSING THEIR SUPERPOWER AS IMPOTENT AND INEPT.

THE FRENCH AND GERMANS ARE PISSED OFF TOO.

GOD **DAMN** IT! I WANT THAT KID BACK HERE!

EVO MORALES
PRESIDENT OF BOLIVIA

OBAMA'S PANIC LED TO AT LEAST ONE ASTONISHING BREACH OF INTERNATIONAL PROTOCOL. PRESIDENT EVO MORALES OF BOLIVIA WAS FLYING BACK FROM A SUMMIT IN MOSCOW ON JULY 2.

ACTING ON A TIP THAT MORALES WAS SMUGGLING SNOWDEN TO ASYLUM, THE U.S. ASKED ITS EUROPEAN ALLIES TO REVOKE THEIR FLYOVER PERMISSION. THE PLANE WAS FORCED TO LAND IN AUSTRIA AND SEARCHED. NO SNOWDEN.

IN MOSCOW, INTELLIGENCE AGENTS
FOR THE FSB -- SUCCESSOR OF THE
SOVIET KGB -- TURNED UP TO SEE IF
THEY MIGHT CONVINCE SNOWDEN TO
GIVE INFORMATION ABOUT THE NSA
TO THE RUSSIAN GOVERNMENT.

SNOWDEN REFUSED.

SNOWDEN DECIDED TO HOLD HIS FIRST PRESS CONFERENCE IN THE TRANSIT AREA OF THE MOSCOW AIRPORT. HE ELOQUENTLY DEFENDED HIS ACTIONS, QUOTING THE NUREMBERG TRIBUNAL'S REBUKE TO THE NAZI WAR CRIMINALS WHO CLAIMED THEY WERE "JUST FOLLOWING ORDERS":

"INDIVIDUALS HAVE INTERNATIONAL DUTIES WHICH TRANSCEND THE NATIONAL OBLIGATIONS OF OBEDIENCE."

I DID WHAT I BELIEVED WAS RIGHT AND BEGAN A CAMPAIGN TO CORRECT THIS WRONGDOING. I DID NOT SEEK TO ENRICH MYSELF.

INDEED, HE COULD HAVE SOLD THE NSA DOCUMENTS TO A FOREIGN SPY AGENCY. ROBERT HANSSEN AND ALDRICH AMES, WHO HELD HIGH-RANKING POSTS IN THE FBI AND CIA, DID THAT.

ROBT. HANSSEN
FBI AGENT:
PAID $1.4 MILLION

ALDRICH AMES
CIA OFFICER:
PAID $4.6 MILLION

I DID NOT PARTNER WITH ANY FOREIGN GOVERNMENT TO GUARANTEE MY SAFETY.

THIS IS LESS CLEAR. HE REQUESTED ASYLUM FROM 20 NATIONS, AND NOW RELIES ON RENEWABLE RESIDENCY PERMITS THAT ALLOW HIM TO REMAIN IN RUSSIA.

To: Federal Migration Com
of the Russian Fed.
From- Edward J. Snowden
United States Citizen

APPLICATION

I hereby request your
considering the possibility
of granting me temporary

"INSTEAD, I TOOK WHAT I KNEW TO THE PUBLIC, SO WHAT AFFECTS ALL OF US CAN BE DISCUSSED BY ALL OF US **IN THE LIGHT OF DAY**, AND I ASKED THE WORLD FOR JUSTICE."

" THAT MORAL DECISION TO TELL THE PUBLIC ABOUT SPYING THAT AFFECTS ALL OF US HAS BEEN COSTLY, BUT IT WAS THE RIGHT THING TO DO."

SOME PEOPLE ARGUE THAT PRIVACY ISN'T IMPORTANT, OR THAT IT'S A THING OF THE PAST IN THE DIGITAL AGE. BUT PRIVACY IS TOO IMPORTANT TO GIVE UP ON.

CONSERVATIVE *NEW YORK TIMES* COLUMNIST DAVID BROOKS IS OFTEN WRONG. YET HE'S GOOD AT EXPLAINING THE VALUE OF PRIVACY:

"THERE HAS TO BE AN INTERIOR ZONE WITHIN EACH PERSON THAT OTHER PEOPLE DON'T SEE. THERE HAS TO BE A ZONE WHERE HALF-FORMED THOUGHTS AND DELICATE EMOTIONS CAN GROW AND EVOLVE, WITHOUT BEING EXPOSED TO THE HARSH GLARE OF PUBLIC JUDGMENT...THERE HAS TO BE A PRIVATE SPACE WHERE YOU CAN SHARE YOUR DOUBTS AND SECRETS AND EXPOSE YOUR WEAKNESSES WITH THE EXPECTATION THAT YOU WILL STILL BE LOVED AND FORGIVEN AND SUPPORTED."

IF SOMEONE IS LISTENING TO EVERYTHING YOU SAY -- SOMEONE POWERFUL -- YOU WON'T EVOLVE.

THEN THERE'S THE PROBLEM OF
STATE CONTROL. HOW CAN ANYONE
FEEL SAFE KNOWING THAT THE
GOVERNMENT -- ANY GOVERNMENT,
EVEN A RELATIVELY BENEVOLENT
GOVERNMENT (FOR NOW) -- KNOWS
EVERYTHING ABOUT THEM?

HISTORY SHOWS THAT, SOONER
RATHER THAN LATER, OFFICIALS
AND INSTITUTIONS THAT KNOW
EVERYTHING ABOUT THEIR CITIZENS
USE THAT KNOWLEDGE TO
CONTROL THEM.

EVEN IF YOU TRUST THE GOVERNMENT AND YOU AGREE WITH THE NSA AND ITS ACTIONS, THERE'S THE QUESTION OF ACCOUNTABILITY.

LIKE IT OR NOT, NSA OFFICIALS BROKE FEDERAL LAW. THEY VIOLATED OUR CONSTITUTIONAL RIGHTS. SOME EVEN LIED UNDER OATH, TO CONGRESS. WE COULD LEGALIZE NSA SPYING...BUT THAT DOESN'T ALTER THE FACT THAT IT IS ILLEGAL NOW. THOSE WHO BREAK THE LAW NOW SHOULD BE PUNISHED. SNOWDEN? PERHAPS. JAMES CLAPPER, KEITH ALEXANDER, BARACK OBAMA, GEORGE W. BUSH, FOR SURE.

FINALLY, IN LATE JULY 2013,
EDWARD SNOWDEN MOVED INTO
TEMPORARY HOUSING, A MODEST
HOUSE IN THE SUBURBS OF
MOSCOW.

SNOWDEN'S GIRLFRIEND, LINDSAY
MILLS, JOINED HIM IN JULY 2014.

THEY WERE PHOTOGRAPHED
ATTENDING THE OPERA.

THEY LOOKED HAPPY.

THERE HAVE BEEN REPORTS THAT
EDWARD SNOWDEN WORKS AS A
COMPUTER PROGRAMMER.

THIS SEEMS UNLIKELY. HE HAS
COUNTLESS INTERVIEW REQUESTS
TO KEEP HIM BUSY.

WILL HE EVER RETURN TO THE
UNITED STATES? PERHAPS. HE HAS
SAID THAT HE WOULD WILLINGLY
COME HOME TO FACE A "FAIR
TRIAL," WHATEVER THAT MEANS. IT
IS DOUBTFUL THAT HE WOULD GET
ONE.

THERE IS LITTLE REASON TO BELIEVE
THAT THE CHARGES AGAINST HIM
WILL BE DROPPED, OR THAT HE WILL
RECEIVE A PARDON ANY TIME
SOON.

DOES SNOWDEN UNDERSTAND
THAT? HE MUST.

IF NOT, THAT'S THE FORMER BOY
SCOUT IN HIM.

MEANWHILE, THE DEBATE HAS BECOME PERSONAL -- ABOUT SNOWDEN HIMSELF MORE THAN THE ISSUES TO WHICH HE HOPED TO DRAW ATTENTION.

IT ISN'T SURPRISING THAT SOME AMERICANS ARE SUSPICIOUS OF SNOWDEN'S MOTIVES. HIS STORY SEEMS ALMOST TOO GOOD TO BE TRUE: A YOUNG MAN OF MODEST MEANS, PROPELLED BY HIS BRILLIANCE TO A POSITION THAT GAVE HIM UNUSUAL ACCESS TO THE NATION'S MOST CLOSELY GUARDED SECRETS...

THEN, IN THE FINEST TRADITION OF POLITICAL THRILLERS LIKE *ALL THE PRESIDENT'S MEN* AND *ENEMY OF THE STATE,* THE FORMER BOY SCOUT GOES PUBLIC SO CITIZENS CAN RESTORE A NATION WHERE PERSONAL FREEDOM AND PRIVACY RIGHTS ARE RESPECTED.

AS HIS CRITICS POINT OUT, SNOWDEN BROKE THE LAW.

IT'S ALSO TRUE THAT HE VIOLATED HIS PROMISE, WHICH HE MADE VOLUNTARILY, NOT TO REVEAL THE NATION'S SECRETS. AND WHEN HE WENT TO BOOZ ALLEN HAMILTON, IT WAS WITH THE EXPRESS PURPOSE OF SPYING ON THE SPIES SO HE COULD STEAL THEIR SECRETS AND GIVE THEM TO THE WORLD.

BUT THIS IS A CASE WHERE LAWS CONFLICT. WHICH MATTER MORE?

THE GOVERNMENT'S SECRETS? OR OURS?

THE NSA IS A MILITARY-TYPE
HIERARCHY. IF ANY AGENT CAN GO
ROGUE ANY TIME, SNOWDEN'S CRITICS
SAY, CHAOS WILL REIGN: THE SYSTEM
WILL FALL APART. THEN THERE'S THE
LEGACY OF NUREMBERG: SOME
SYSTEMS *SHOULD* BE UNDERMINED.

THE GOVERNMENT CLAIMS THAT THE NSA IS ALL ABOUT UNCOVERING TERRORIST PLOTS; INDEED, IT WAS ROUNDLY CRITICIZED FOR NOT PREVENTING THE 9/11 ATTACKS. THE NSA CLAIMED ITS PRISM PROGRAM SAVED MANY LIVES. IF THAT'S TRUE, SOME PEOPLE ASK, AND IF ONE OF THOSE SAVED LIVES IS YOURS OR THAT OF SOMEONE YOU LOVE, ISN'T IT WORTH IT TO SWEEP UP METADATA?

WE KNOW OF AT LEAST **50** THREATS THAT HAVE BEEN AVERTED BECAUSE OF THAT INFORM-ATION... SO LIVES HAVE BEEN SAVED.*

* Still no evidence of this.

WHERE YOU STAND ON SNOWDEN
TENDS TO BE LINKED TO HOW MUCH
YOU TRUST THE GOVERNMENT.

IF YOU SEE THE U.S. GOVERNMENT AS A
FLAWED INSTITUTION THAT EMPLOYS
PATRIOTIC PEOPLE TRYING TO DO
THEIR BEST TO KEEP THE COUNTRY
SAFE AND STRONG, YOU'RE
LIKELY TO TAKE POLITICIANS AT THEIR
WORD WHEN THEY SAY THEY DON'T
ABUSE THEIR POWER, THAT THEIR
SURVEILLANCE TARGETS ARE ALL
TERRORISTS.

IF, ON THE OTHER HAND, YOU SEE THE UNITED STATES AS A MILITARISTIC EMPIRE OUT TO CONQUER MOST OF THE WORLD AND DOMINATE THE REST, DEFINED BY A LONG HISTORY OF GENOCIDE, SYSTEMIC RACISM, AND RUTHLESS SUPPRESSION OF DISSENT, THEN YOU PROBABLY THINK THAT THE GOVERNMENT CAN'T BE TRUSTED.

IT HELPS TO UNDERSTAND THAT SNOWDEN WASN'T FOLLOWING THE BABY BOOMER MODEL OF THE CIVIL DISOBEDIENCE MARTYR, BUT THE GEN X EXAMPLE OF THE PRAGMATIC ACTIVIST. SNOWDEN'S STRATEGY WAS TO WORK WITH ESTABLISHED MEDIA ORGANIZATIONS.

LIKE JULIAN ASSANGE, HE WAS DETERMINED TO STAY OUT OF JAIL -- AND BECOME AN EXPLAINER, A SPOKESPERSON FOR A CAUSE THAT DESPERATELY NEEDS ONE.

WE SING THAT WE LIVE IN THE LAND OF THE FREE AND THE BRAVE, BUT THAT'S A LIE. MOST OF US DO WHAT WE'RE TOLD.

IS IT POSSIBLE THAT, OF THE THOUSANDS OF EMPLOYEES OF THE NSA WITH ACCESS TO THE SAME INFORMATION, THEY WERE ALL WRONG BECAUSE THEY DIDN'T SPEAK OUT, AND ONLY ONE PERSON -- SNOWDEN -- WAS RIGHT?

YEAH. IT IS.

SNOWDEN SAYS HE HAS NO REGRETS.

YET IT'S NORMAL FOR US TO SECOND-GUESS HIM, ETHICALLY AS WELL AS TACTICALLY. WOULD I HAVE SPOKEN UP? WOULD YOU HAVE?

WOULD WE HAVE AIRED OUR COMPLAINTS WITHIN THE SYSTEM, PERHAPS WITH A LETTER TO A MEMBER OF CONGRESS?

OR WOULD WE HAVE KEPT SILENT?

I KNOW THAT IN SNOWDEN'S POSITION I WOULD HAVE DONE THE SAME THING. BUT I WOULD NEVER HAVE TAKEN A JOB LIKE WORKING FOR THE NSA OR THE CIA IN THE FIRST PLACE.

THIS IS WHY SNOWDEN IS UNIQUE: IN AN ORGANIZATION THAT SELECTS FOR UNTHINKING CONFORMISTS, HE SEARCHED FOR TRUTH AND FOLLOWED IT TO AN IDEOLOGICAL AWAKENING.
ONLY SNOWDEN COULD BLOW THE WHISTLE ON THE NSA.

SNOWDEN DID THE RIGHT THING. WHAT THE NSA WAS DOING BRAZENLY VIOLATED ITS OWN CHARTER.

THE NSA MAKES ME AFRAID OF "MY" GOVERNMENT.

WE NEED TO KNOW WHAT THEY ARE DOING.

SNOWDEN ASYLUM?

AS THE LEFTIST GOVERNMENT OF BRAZIL CONSIDERS SNOWDEN'S ASYLUM REQUEST, NEWS ABOUT NSA SPYING ON BRAZIL IS BREAKING...

IT'S OUR INFORMATION, AND THEY'RE
STEALING IT. AND THEY'RE SPENDING
OUR TAX DOLLARS TO DO IT.

NSA DEFENDERS SAY PRIVACY WAS
ALREADY DEAD, THAT WE SHARE OUR
PRIVATE LIVES WITH PRIVATE
CORPORATIONS. BUT NO CORPORATION
HAS EVER KICKED DOWN PEOPLE'S
DOORS, SHOVED THEM INTO TRAINS,
AND SHIPPED THEM TO CONCENTRATION
CAMPS.

ONLY GOVERNMENTS HAVE DONE THAT.

WE NEED RULES THAT LIMIT
OUR LEADERS' POWERS MORE
THAN WE NEED RULES THAT
LIMIT OUR RIGHTS.

THE AMERICAN NEWS MEDIA TENDS
TO FOCUS ITS COVERAGE ON
PERSONALITIES RATHER THAN ISSUES.
TRUE TO FORM, REPORTING ABOUT
THE SNOWDEN LEAKS OBSESSED
OVER HIS PERSONALITY AND THE
SIMPLISTIC BINARY QUESTION OF
WHETHER HE IS A TRAITOR OR A
HERO. GOVERNMENT SPYING ON
AMERICANS GOT RELATIVELY LITTLE
ATTENTION.

**Plurality of Younger Americans Say Edward
Snowden is a Patriot; Majority of Seniors
Say He's a Traitor**

*Would you say that Edward Snowden is a patriot
for letting the public know about the government's
surveillance of Americans, or that he is a traitor for
leaking government secrets to the media whose
reports are seen by America's enemies?*

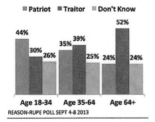

REASON-RUPE POLL SEPT 4-8 2013

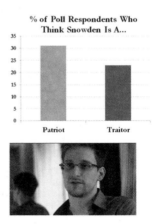

BY THE TIME THE 2016 PRESIDENTIAL
CAMPAIGN GOT UNDERWAY, THE
ISSUE OF PRIVACY HAD ALL BUT
VANISHED FROM THE POLITICAL
SCENE.

NEVERTHELESS, THE OBAMA ADMINISTRATION CAME UNDER PRESSURE TO RESPOND, OR APPEAR TO RESPOND. THE RESULT WAS THE "USA FREEDOM ACT" (A PLAY ON THE USA PATRIOT ACT, WHOSE SECTION 215 HAD AUTHORIZED EXPANDED NSA SURVEILLANCE).

"To rein in the dragnet collection of data by the National Security Agency (NSA) and other government agencies, increase transparency of the Foreign Intelligence Surveillance Court (FISC), provide businesses the ability to release information regarding FISA requests, and create an independent constitutional advocate to argue cases before the FISC."

—Rep. Jim Sensenbrenner, introducing the bill.

CRITICS LIKE THE ELECTRONIC FRONTIER FOUNDATION CALLED THE VERSION OF THE BILL THAT CAME OUT OF CONGRESS "WATERED DOWN." MANY IN CONGRESS WANTED TO RENEW THE USA PATRIOT ACT AS IS.

IN MAY 2015, A FEDERAL APPEALS
COURT ISSUED THE FIRST JUDICIAL
ASSESSMENT OF THE NSA'S POST-9/11
ACTIVITIES. THE COURT RULED THAT
THE BULK COLLECTION OF
TELEPHONY METADATA -- THE FIRST
PROGRAM REVEALED BY SNOWDEN --
WAS UNLAWFUL.

Edward Snowden fans see vindication in court ruling

New York court's ruling says that the NSA surveillance Snowden exposed was "illegal."

By **NAHAL TOOSI** and **JOSH GERSTEIN** | 5/7/15 3:25 PM EDT | Updated 5/8/15 6:20 AM EDT

Edward Snowden hasn't had his day in court, but he's already finding some vindication in the U.S. judicial system.

A U.S. appeals court's ruling on Thursday that bulk collection of telephone metadata by the National Security Agency is illegal has given fresh hope to supporters of the

SNOWDEN WAS VINDICATED.

BUT THE VICTORY WAS LARGELY
SYMBOLIC.

THE COURT DIDN'T ORDER THE NSA
TO STOP. THE GOVERNMENT WILL
APPEAL. THE COURT DIDN'T SAY
THAT THE NSA'S ACTIONS WERE
UNCONSTITUTIONAL VIOLATIONS OF
AMERICANS' RIGHT TO BE FREE FROM
UNREASONABLE SEARCH AND SEIZURE.

FOR THE TIMEBEING, IT'S BUSINESS AS USUAL AT THE NSA, BUT THAT DOESN'T MEAN NOTHING HAS CHANGED. THE GOVERNMENTS AND CITIZENS OF OTHER COUNTRIES ARE STILL THINKING, TALKING, AND REACTING.

MOSTLY, THEY'RE WALKING AWAY FROM U.S. TECH COMPANIES.

TECHNOLOGY & MEDIA

NSA Spying Scandal Could Cost U.S. Tech Giants Billions

AT&T and Verizon have remained silent about their role in the NSA's programs

The National Security Agency spying scandal could cost the top U.S. tech companies billions of dollars over the next several years, according to industry experts. In addition to consumer Internet companies, hardware and cloud-storage giants like IBM, Hewlett-Packard, and Oracle could suffer

THE IMPLICATIONS ARE HUGE. FOR EXAMPLE, EUROPEAN NATIONS AND BUSINESSES, WORRIED THAT THE CURRENT ITERATION OF THE "CLOUD" HAS BEEN COMPROMISED BY THE NSA, ARE WORKING ON A "EURO-CLOUD."

CloudforEurope

FRANCE EVEN PASSED A LAW MAKING IT LEGAL FOR A FRENCH INTELLIGENCE AGENT TO EXPOSE WRONGDOING WITHIN THE SECURITY SERVICES.

The Washington Post

WorldViews

France's National Assembly shows support for legalization of Edward Snowden-style whistleblowing

By Rick Noack April 1)

ON THE OTHER HAND...

english

Why America is Not Norma

These 8 facts prove the situation in America is not right

● ○

FRANCE - Article published the Monday 13 April 2015 - Latest update : Monday 13 April 2015

France's new spy bill raises fears of mass surveillance

By Mike Woods

A bill proposing a controversial set of new intelligence-gathering measures entered into a fast-tracked debate in France's parliament on Monday. Both the government and main opposition parties support the bill

"SOONER RATHER THAN LATER, THE WEB IS GOING TO GO DARK," A SOURCE WHO CURRENTLY WORKS AT THE NSA TOLD ME. THIS IS THE INTELLIGENCE COMMUNITY'S WORST NIGHTMARE.

I ASKED: "BECAUSE EVERYONE WILL BE USING SOLID ENCRYPTION?"

"YES, WE WON'T BE ABLE TO SEE ANYTHING."

"Encryption is nothing new. But the challenge to law enforcement and national security officials is markedly worse, with recent default encryption settings and encrypted devices and networks — all designed to increase security and privacy."

—FBI director James Comey

A FREE-MARKET SOLUTION. SNOWDEN THE LIBERTARIAN HAS TO LIKE THAT.

NSA SPYING IS NO LONGER AT THE TOP OF THE HEADLINES, BUT MANY AMERICANS ARE STILL GRATEFUL TO THE NSA WHISTLEBLOWER.

SNOWDEN

IN APRIL 2015 AN UNKNOWN ARTIST ADDED A BRONZE BUST OF SNOWDEN TO A WAR MEMORIAL IN BROOKLYN. IT WAS THE SECOND SUCH STATUE IN A NEW YORK PARK -- AND ACTIVISTS DEMANDED THAT THE COPS WHO TOOK IT AWAY PUT IT BACK.

HOWEVER, MANY AMERICANS --
PERHAPS DUE TO THEIR LACK OF
EXPERIENCE LIVING UNDER A MORE
OPPRESSIVE FORM OF
GOVERNMENT -- THINK THAT IF
YOU HAVE NOTHING TO HIDE, THEN
YOU HAVE NOTHING TO FEAR.
WHICH, NOW, MAY WELL BE TRUE.

BUT GOVERNMENTS CHANGE.

ALL IT TAKES FOR A SOCIETY TO
CLAMP DOWN ON OUR FREEDOM IS
A SINGLE TRAUMATIC EVENT.

WE ALREADY LIVE IN OCEANIA. BUT THAT DOESN'T MEAN 1984 CAN'T GET A LOT WORSE.

AFTER ALL, THE TECHNOLOGICAL, LEGAL, AND POLITICAL INFRASTRUCTURE IS ALREADY IN PLACE.

ON THE OTHER HAND, THERE ARE REASONS TO BE HOPEFUL. IN APRIL 2015, A CLASSIFIED GOVERNMENT REVIEW OF "STELLARWIND," THE NSA PROGRAM THAT SWEPT UP BULK METADATA OF PHONE CALLS, FOUND THAT IT WASN'T USEFUL IN TRACKING TERRORISTS BECAUSE IT WAS TOO SECRET: TOO FEW WORKING-LEVEL CIA AGENTS KNEW ABOUT IT.

IRONIC!

(U//FOUO) Evolution of NSA Partnerships with Private Sector

(U) History of NSA Partnerships with Private Sector

(TS//SI//NF) As far back as World War II, NSA has had classified relationships with carefully vetted U.S. companies that assist with essential foreign intelligence-gathering activities. NSA maintains relationships with over 100 U.S. companies. Without their cooperation, NSA would not be able respond to intelligence requirements on a variety of topics important ... United States.

(U) Access to Program Information

(TS//SI//STLW//NF) Between 4 October 2001 and 17 January 2007, NSA cleared over 3,000 people for the PSP. The majority worked at NSA. Others were from the CIA, the FBI, the Department of Justice, Congress, the FISC, the ODNI, the White House, and the DoD.

(TS//SI//STLW//NF) PSP Clearance Totals

Agency	Number of Cleared Personnel
NSA	1,936

THE FBI DETERMINED THAT, IN THE THREE YEARS AFTER 9/11, ONLY 1.2% OF STELLARWIND TIPS PANNED OUT.

PUBLIC APPROVAL OF THE NSA HAS PLUMMETED SINCE THE SNOWDEN REVELATIONS.

AT THE TIME OF THE LEAKS, 56% OF AMERICANS TOLD THE PEW POLL THEY APPROVED OF THE NSA. BY LATE 2014, 80% DISAPPROVED.

Public Increasingly Wary of the NSA, Poll Finds

NOVEMBER 12, 2014   BY PATRICK TUCKER
The NSA's PR outreach just got a lot harder. By Patrick Tucker   Cyber   ⁄ Intelligence ⌄

January 20, 2014, 03:36 pm
Poll: Public turning against NSA practices

Poll: Most Americans now oppose the NSA program

Poll: Only 11 percent believe Obama's NSA promises

THE NSA SCARES PEOPLE SO MUCH THAT MOST OF THEM REFUSE TO ANSWER QUESTIONS ABOUT THE AGENCY VIA THE INTERNET FOR FEAR OF BEING MONITORED.

> WELL AWARE THAT THEY'RE ON THE POLITICAL ROPES BECAUSE PEOPLE DON'T LIKE THEM, NSA OFFICIALS ARE RESORTING TO A CHARM OFFENSIVE THAT EXPOSES THEIR DESPERATION.

White House Takes Cybersecurity Pitch to Silicon Valley

By DAVID E. SANGER and NICOLE PERLROTH   APRIL 26, 2015

SAN FRANCISCO — President Obama's newly installed defense secretary, Ashton B. Carter, toured Silicon Valley last week to announce a new military strategy for computer conflict, starting the latest Pentagon effort to invest in promising start-ups and to meet with engineers whose talent he declared the Pentagon desperately needed in fending off the nation's adversaries.

Mr. Carter immediately acknowledged, though, the need to rebuild trust with Silicon Valley, whose mainstays — like Apple, Google and Facebook (whose new headquarters he toured) have spent two years demonstrating to customers around the world that they are rolling out encryption technologies to defeat surveillance. That, of course, includes blocking the National Security Agency, a critical member of the military-intelligence community.

Not long after Mr. Johnson declared that "encryption is making it harder for your government to find criminal activity and potential terrorist activity," large numbers of entrepreneurs and engineers crammed into the first of several seminars, called "Post-Snowden Cryptography." There, they took notes as the world's best code makers mocked the Obama administration's drive for a "technical compromise" that would ensure the government some continued access.

FOLLOWING POET WILLIAM ROSS
WALLACE'S DICTUM THAT "THE
HAND THAT ROCKS THE CRADLE IS
THE HAND THAT RULES THE
WORLD," THE NSA HAS EVEN
DEPLOYED LOW-QUALITY
PROPAGANDA, SIMILAR TO WHAT
THIRD-WORLD DICTATORSHIPS USE
IN ORDER TO BRAINWASH CHILDREN.

Crypto Cat
Information Assurance Analyst
The purrr-fect little feline, she lo
secret messages to purrr-plex h

HERE'S THE KIDS' SECTION OF THE NSA WEBSITE!

THEY KNOW THEY'RE IN TROUBLE.

IN APRIL 2015, AS SNOWDEN FACED
HIS THIRD YEAR IN EXILE,
INTERVIEWER JOHN OLIVER ASKED
HIM IF HE WAS HOMESICK.

"I DO MISS MY COUNTRY. I DO
MISS MY HOME. I DO MISS MY
FAMILY," HE REPLIED.

THAT WAS THE SOUNDBYTE.

BEFORE THAT EDWARD SNOWDEN ANSWERED JOHN OLIVER'S QUESTION WITH OTHER WORDS THAT WEREN'T QUOTED IN THE MEDIA:

MY COUNTRY IS SOMETHING THAT TRAVELS WITH ME. IT'S NOT JUST A GEOGRAPHICAL LOCATION.

TED RALL

Afterword

Vindication of Edward Snowden's actions came in the form of a court decision[*] and congressional action. In May 2015 a federal appeals panel in New York became the first court to consider the legality of one of the National Security Agency programs leaked by Snowden, which carry out bulk surveillance of the American people. Though the government is certain to appeal, the court's decision was a clear rebuke to the NSA and the Obama administration. Even under the notorious Section 215 of the USA Patriot Act, the gathering of "telephony metadata"—times, places, and numbers of both ends of phone calls—is illegal, the judges ruled.

The decision breathed new life into the USA Freedom Act,[**] a bill designed to curtail the NSA's telephony metadata program, called "Stellar Wind." Thanks to a coalition of libertarian-minded Republicans like Rand Paul and traditional liberal Democrats, a reform believed doomed seemed likelier to bring about the first legislative rollback of government intrusiveness since 9/11.

This was good news for privacy, and thus for our basic rights as citizens. But I'm struck by how limited the debate over the Snowden leaks has been since he stepped out of the shadows.

The NSA's telephony metadata program was the first story revealed by Snowden and *Guardian* columnist Glenn Greenwald[***] from their Hong Kong hotel room in June 2013. So far, it's the only NSA leak to have received extensive coverage from U.S. state-controlled media—and the only program to have been addressed by the legislative and judicial branches of the political system.

But that's just the tip of the iceberg when it comes to NSA spying on Americans. Snowden took tens of thousands of

---

[*] http://www.cnn.com/2015/05/07/politics/nsa-telephone-metadata-illegal-court
[**] https://firstlook.org/theintercept/2015/05/19/patriot-act-debate-capitol-hill-fiery-drama-bound-end-whimper/
[***] http://www.theguardian.com/world/2013/jun/06/nsa-phone-records-verizon-court-order

top-secret documents, which reveal numerous active domestic surveillance sweeps that are, if anything, even more intrusive and worrisome than telephony metadata.

"The only debate we're really having in the U.S. is about the very first document that Snowden produced," former NSA general counsel Stewart Baker told *The New York Times*.[*] "The rest of the documents have been used as a kind of intelligence porn for the rest of the world—'Oooh, look at what NSA is doing.'"

Baker is an ardent NSA defender who vehemently disagrees that Snowden was right to leak the documentation behind these programs. Ironically, his remarks inadvertently prompt one to ask, why haven't we been talking about these other, even more intrusive, violations of privacy?

Is it the media's notorious inability to sustain focus on stories, especially when they're complicated? Or are they consciously complicit in a conspiracy to keep silent about America's out-of-control security state—nothing to see here, just move on?

Glenn Greenwald, his partner the documentary filmmaker Laura Poitras, and other principals behind First Look Media created *The Intercept* to handle releases of the Snowden files, hoping that the "drip drip drip" effect of one revelation after another after another would become impossible for the Obama administration and its allies to withstand. It was a smart strategy, one that I thought would work. But it hasn't turned out that way. Like a dog reduced to whimpering helplessness by sustained abuse,[**] Americans go about their daily lives convinced they can't do a thing about the NSA.

It's important to remember that telephony metadata is only a tiny part of the NSA's war on American privacy. Even total victory—elimination of bulk collection, which is unlikely—would leave many more battles to fight for those who still care about freedom.

---

[*] http://www.nytimes.com/2015/05/20/world/europe/snowden-sees-some-victories-from-a-distance.html?_r=1
[**] http://study.com/academy/lesson/how-seligmans-learned-helplessness-theory-applies-to-human-depression-and-stress.html

Notes

18. "A Shredded Safety Net," by Elizabeth Lower-Basch, *The American Prospect*, May 31, 2013. https://prospect.org/article/shredded-safety-net

19. "Sysadmin Security Fail: NSA finds Snowden Hijacked Officials' Logins," by Sean Gallagher, *Ars Technica*, August 29, 2013. http://arstechnica.com/information-technology/2013/08/sysadmin-security-fail-nsa-finds-snowden-hijacked-officials-logins/

20. "The Most Wanted Man in the World," by James Bamford, *Wired*, August 13, 2014. http://www.wired.com/2014/08/edward-snowden/

22. "The Crux of the NSA Story in One Phrase: 'Collect It All,'" by Glenn Greenwald, *The Guardian*, July 15, 2013. http://www.theguardian.com/commentisfree/2013/jul/15/crux-nsa-collect-it-all

23. "Sens. Ron Wyden (D-Ore., pictured) and Mark Udall (D-Colo.) . . . [said they were] 'barred by Senate rules from commenting on some of the details at this time.' Udall said he 'did everything short of leaking classified information.'" From "These Two Senators Tried to Warn Us About the NSA's Snooping," by Alex Fitzpatrick, Mashable.com, June 7, 2013. http://mashable.com/2013/06/07/wyden-udall-nsa/

24. "Barack Obama on Surveillance, Then and Now," by Caroline Houck, PolitiFact.com, June 13, 2013. http://www.politifact.com/truth-o-meter/article/2013/jun/13/barack-obama-surveillance-then-and-now/

25. "Edward Snowden Blames President Obama," by Tal Kopan, *Politico*, June 18, 2013. http://www.politico.com/story/2013/06/edward-snowden-blames-obama-92901.html

    "Edward Snowden Is a Ron Paul Supporter," by Amanda Terkel, *The Huffington Post*, June 10, 2013. http://www.huffingtonpost.com/2013/06/10/edward-snowden-ron-paul_n_3414992.html

26. "Edward Snowden, NSA files source: 'If They Want To Get You, In Time They Will,'" by Ewen MacAskill, *The Guardian*, June 10, 2013. http://www.theguardian.com/world/2013/jun/09/nsa-whistleblower-edward-snowden-why

    "Edward Snowden Blames President Obama," by Tal Kopan.

27. Putative numbers range from thousands to 1.7 million. We don't know the actual number. "Meet Edward Snowden, the NSA Whistleblower," by Garance Franke-Ruta, *The Atlantic*, June 9, 2013. http://www.theatlantic.com/politics/archive/2013/06/meet-edward-snowden-the-nsa-whistleblower/276688/

    "How Much Did Snowden Take? Not Even the NSA Really Knows," by Joe Kloc, *Newsweek*, June 9, 2014. http://www.newsweek.com/how-much-did-snowden-take-not-even-nsa-really-knows-253940

    "Booz Allen Exec Describes How Snowden Deceived His Former Employer," by Margaret Hartmann, *New York* magazine, February 4, 2014. http://nymag.com/daily/intelligencer/2014/02/booz-allen-exec-describes-how-snowden-did-it.html

28. "If all seemed well, the source would walk past holding a Rubik's Cube." From "How Edward J. Snowden Orchestrated a Blockbuster Story," by Charlie Savage and Mark Mazzetti, *The New York Times*, June 10, 2013. http://www.nytimes.com/2013/06/11/us/how-edward-j-snowden-orchestrated-a-blockbuster-story.html

29. On the left: senator Dianne Feinstein, Democrat of California and chairman of the Senate Intelligence Committee. On the right: German chancellor Angela Merkel. "[Senator Dianne] Feinstein 'Totally Opposed' to Spying on Foreign Leaders," by Ed O'Keefe, *The Washington Post*, October 28, 2013. http://www.washingtonpost.com/blogs/post-politics/wp/2013/10/28/feinstein-totally-opposed-to-spying-on-foreign-leaders/

    "[German chancellor Angela] Merkel Compared NSA to Stasi in Heated Encounter with Obama," by Ian Traynor and Paul Lewis, *The Guardian*, December 17, 2013. http://www.theguardian.com/world/2013/dec/17/merkel-compares-nsa-stasi-obama

German intelligence officers told Merkel the NSA was tapping her personal cell phone. Whether or not it was, the Snowden leaks contributed to an atmosphere of fear and distrust, even between stalwart allies.

See: "German Investigation Says the NSA Probably Didn't Tap Merkel's Phone After All," by Max Fisher, Vox.com, December 12, 2014. http://www.vox.com/2014/12/12/7381539/merkel-phone-tapped-nsa

30. "James Clapper Says He Answered Senator Wyden in the 'Least Untruthful Manner' He Could Think Of," by Dan Amira, New York magazine, June 10, 2013. http://nymag.com/daily/intelligencer/2013/06/clapper-wyden-least-untruthful-too-cute-half.html

33. "FAQ: What You Need to Know About the NSA's Surveillance Programs," by Jonathan Stray, ProPublica, August 5, 2013. http://www.propublica.org/article/nsa-data-collection-faq

"The system can even search for keywords and identify the person speaking if a voice sample of that individual has been stored." From: "How the NSA Helped Turkey Kill Kurdish Rebels," by Laura Poitras, Marcel Rosenbach, Michael Sontheimer, and Holger Stark, The Intercept, August 31, 2014. https://firstlook.org/theintercept/2014/08/31/nsaturkeyspiegel

34. "'You're the bomb!' Are You at Risk from the Anti-terrorism Algorithms?," by James Ball, The Guardian, December 2, 2014. http://www.theguardian.com/uk-news/2014/dec/02/youre-the-bomb-are-you-at-risk-from-anti-terrorism-algorithms-automated-tracking-innocent-people

"These Are Supposedly The Words That Make the NSA Think You're a Terrorist," by Dylan Love, Business Insider, June 13, 2013. http://www.businessinsider.com/nsa-prism-keywords-for-domestic-spying-2013-6

"The New Technology at the Root of the NSA Wiretap Scandal," by Jon Stokes, Ars Technica, December 20, 2005. http://arstechnica.com/uncategorized/2005/12/20/5808-2/

35. "T-Mobile, Verizon Wireless Shielded from NSA," by Danny Yadron and Evan Perez, The Wall Street Journal, June 14, 2013. http://www.wsj.com/article_email/SB1000142412788732404950457854380024026636 8-lMyQjAxMTAzMDEwMzExNDMyWj.html

"The NSA Has Processed 1 TRILLION Pieces of Internet Metadata — And That's Just The Start," by Michael B. Kelley, Business Insider, June 28, 2013. http://www.businessinsider.com/nsa-processed-1-trillion-pieces-of-data-2013-6

36. "Whistleblower: NSA Stores 80% of All Phone Calls, Not Just Metadata—Full Audio," RT, July 12, 2014. http://rt.com/news/172284-nsa-stores-calls-audio/

ACLU attorney Ben Wizner, who represents Edward Snowden, questions the 80 percent claim about the U.S. in notes to the publisher.

"NSA Surveillance Program Reaches 'Into the Past' to Retrieve, Replay Phone Calls," by Barton Gellman and Ashkan Soltani, The Washington Post, March 18, 2014. http://www.washingtonpost.com/world/national-security/nsa-surveillance-program-reaches-into-the-past-to-retrieve-replay-phone-calls/2014/03/18/226d2646-ade9-11e3-a49e-76adc9210f19_story.html

37. "The system has the capacity to reach roughly 75 percent of all U.S. Internet traffic in the hunt for foreign intelligence, including a wide array of communications by foreigners and Americans. In some cases, it retains the written content of emails sent between citizens within the U.S. and also filters domestic phone calls made with Internet technology, these people say." From "New Details Show Broader NSA Surveillance Reach," by Siobhan Gorman and Jennifer Valentino-Devries, The Wall Street Journal, August 20, 2013. http://www.wsj.com/articles/SB10001424127887324108204579022874091732470

41. The original NSA charter: https://w2.eff.org/Privacy/Key_escrow/Clipper/nsa.charter

"The Foreign Intelligence Surveillance Act forbids the NSA from targeting U.S. citizens or legal residents without an order issued by the Foreign Intelligence Surveillance Court. This applies whether the person is in the United States or overseas . . . [If] agency employees pick up the communications of Americans incidentally while monitoring foreign targets, they are supposed to destroy the information unless it contains 'significant foreign intelligence' or evidence of a crime." From "Five Myths about the National Security Agency," by James Bamford, The Washington Post, June 21, 2013. http://www.washingtonpost.com/opinions/five-myths-about-the-national-security-agency/2013/06/21/438e0c4a-d37f-11e2-b05f-3ea3f0e7bb5a_story.html

42. "James Clapper's 'Least Untruthful' Statement to the Senate," by Glenn Kessler, *The Wash-ington Post*, June 12, 2013. http://www.washingtonpost.com/blogs/fact-checker/post/james-clappers-least-untruthful-statement-to-the-senate/2013/06/11/e50677a8-d2d8-11e2-a73e-826d299ff459_blog.html

"In NSA-intercepted Data, Those Not Targeted Far Outnumber the Foreigners Who Are," by Barton Gellman, Julie Tate, and Ashkan Soltani, *The Washington Post*, July 5, 2014. http://www.washingtonpost.com/world/national-security/in-nsa-intercepted-data-those-not-targeted-far-outnumber-the-foreigners-who-are/2014/07/05/8139adf8-045a-11e4-8572-4b1b969b6322_story.html

43. "How to Keep the NSA From Spying Through Your Webcam," by Kim Zetter, *Wired*, March 13, 2014. http://www.wired.com/2014/03/webcams-mics/

44. "How the NSA Plans to Infect 'Millions' of Computers with Malware," by Ryan Gallagher and Glenn Greenwald, *The Intercept*, March 12, 2014. https://firstlook.org/theintercept/2014/03/12/nsa-plans-infect-millions-computers-malware/

"Edward Snowden has revealed that he witnessed 'numerous instances' of National Security Agency (NSA) employees passing around nude photos that were intercepted 'in the course of their daily work.'" From "Snowden: NSA Employees Routinely Pass Around Intercepted Nude Photos," by Cyrus Farivar, *Ars Technica*, July 17, 2014. http://arstechnica.com/tech-policy/2014/07/snowden-nsa-employees-routinely-pass-around-intercepted-nude-photos/

The Agency's interest in sex extends beyond mere prurience to attempts to blackmail and discredit political opponents of the government, especially conservative Muslims, by threatening to publicly reveal the intimate details of their sex lives: "The NSA document, dated Oct. 3, 2012, repeatedly refers to the power of charges of hypocrisy to such a messenger. 'A previous SIGINT'"—or signals intelligence, *the* interception of communications—"'assessment report on radicalization indicated that radicalizers appear to be particularly vulnerable in the area of authority when their private and public behaviors are not consistent,' the document argues.

"Among the vulnerabilities listed by the NSA that can be effectively exploited are 'viewing sexually explicit material online' and 'using sexually explicit persuasive language when communi-cating with inexperienced young girls.'

"According to the document, the NSA believes that exploiting electronic surveillance to publicly reveal online sexual activities can make it harder for these 'radicalizers' to maintain their credibility. 'Focusing on access reveals potential vulnerabilities that could be even more effectively exploited when used in combination with vulnerabilities of character or credibility, or both, of the message in order to shape the perception of the messenger as well as that of his followers,' the document argues.

"An attached appendix lists the 'argument' each surveillance target has made that the NSA says constitutes radicalism, as well the personal 'vulnerabilities' the agency believes would leave the targets 'open to credibility challenges' if exposed.

"One target's offending argument is that 'Non-Muslims are a threat to Islam,' and a vul-nerability listed against him is 'online promiscuity.' Another target, a foreign citizen the NSA describes as a 'respected academic,' holds the offending view that 'offensive jihad is justified,' and his vulnerabilities are listed as 'online promiscuity' and 'publishes articles without checking facts.' A third targeted radical is described as a 'well-known media celebrity' based in the Middle East who argues that 'the U.S. perpetrated the 9/11 attack.' Under vulnerabilities, he is said to lead 'a glamorous lifestyle.' A fourth target, who argues that 'the U.S. brought the 9/11 attacks on itself' is said to be vulnerable to accusations of 'deceitful use of funds.' The document expresses the hope that revealing damaging information about the individuals could undermine their per-ceived 'devotion to the jihadist cause.' From: "Top-Secret Document Reveals NSA Spied on Porn Habits as Part of Plan to Discredit 'Radicalizers,'" by Glenn Greenwald, Ryan Grim, and Ryan Gallagher, *The Huffington Post*, November 26, 2013. http://www.huffingtonpost.com/2013/11/26/nsa-porn-muslims_n_4346128.html

45. "Is Your TV Watching You?" by John R. Quain, Fox News, August 6, 2013. http://www.foxnews.com/tech/2013/08/06/is-your-tv-watching/

46. "NSA Prism Program Taps in to User Data of Apple, Google and Others," by Glenn Greenwald and Ewen MacAskill, *The Guardian*, June 7, 2013. http://www.theguardian.com/world/2013/jun/06/us-tech-giants-nsa-data

    "NSA Leak Vindicates AT&T Whistleblower," by David Kravets, *Wired*, June 27, 2013. http://www.wired.com/2013/06/nsa-whistleblower-klein/

47. "Edward Snowden, NSA files source: 'If They Want To Get You, In Time They Will,'" by Ewen MacAskill.

48. "NSA Whistleblower Reveals Himself: 'I Don't Want to Live in a Society that Does These Sort of Things,'" by Russell Brandom, *The Verge*, June 9, 2013. http://www.theverge.com/2013/6/9/4412080/edward-snowden-comes-out-as-nsa-whistleblower-i-dont-want-to-live-in

49. "U.S. Spies on Millions of Drivers," by Devlin Barrett, *The Wall Street Journal*, June 26, 2015. http://www.wsj.com/articles/u-s-spies-on-millions-of-cars-1422314779

    "Cops Are Freaked Out That Congress May Impose License Plate Reader Limits," by Cyrus Farivar, *Ars Technica*, March 15, 2015. http://arstechnica.com/tech-policy/2015/03/cops-are-freaked-out-that-congress-may-impose-license-plate-reader-limits/

50. "You Are Being Tracked," American Civil Liberties Union report, July 2013. https://www.aclu.org/feature/you-are-being-tracked

51. "U.S. Secretly Tracked Billions of Calls for Decades," by Brad Heath, *USA Today*, April 8, 2015. http://www.usatoday.com/story/news/2015/04/07/dea-bulk-telephone-surveillance-operation/70808616/

    "DEA Sued Over Secret Bulk Collection of Americans' Phone Records," by Spencer Ackerman, *The Guardian*, April 8, 2015. http://www.theguardian.com/us-news/2015/apr/08/dea-bulk-collection-phone-records

52. Recent revelations that "the U.S. Postal Service photographs the front and back of all mail sent through the U.S., ostensibly for sorting purposes, has brought new scrutiny to" an obscure surveillance program run by its law enforcement division, the Postal Inspection Service. The program "lets state or federal law enforcement agencies request what's called a 'mail cover,' giving them access to address information from envelopes and packages sent or received by people targeted in criminal investigations, without a search warrant." From "The U.S.'s Century-Old Snail Mail Surveillance Sparks a New Privacy Argument," by Steven Melendez, *Fast Company*, April 22, 2015. http://www.fastcompany.com/3045337/postal-service-surveillance-privacy-snail-mail

    "U.S. Postal Service Logging All Mail for Law Enforcement," by Ron Nixon, *The New York Times*, July 3, 2013. http://www.nytimes.com/2013/07/04/us/monitoring-of-snail-mail.html

53. "Report Reveals Wider Tracking of Mail in U.S.," by Ron Nixon, *The New York Times*, October 28, 2014. http://www.nytimes.com/2014/10/28/us/us-secretly-monitoring-mail-of-thousands.html

54. "Angry Birds and 'Leaky' Phone Apps Targeted by NSA and GCHQ for User Data," by James Ball, *The Guardian*, January 27, 2014. http://www.theguardian.com/world/2014/jan/27/nsa-gchq-smartphone-app-angry-birds-personal-data

    "The Switchboard: NSA Discussed Using Porn Habits to Discredit Muslim Radicals," by Timothy B. Lee, *The Washington Post*, November 27, 2013. http://www.washingtonpost.com/blogs/the-switch/wp/2013/11/27/the-switchboard-nsa-discussed-using-porn-habits-to-discredit-muslim-radicals/

55. "UK Did Not Use PRISM to Dodge British Law, says Hague," by Ian Evans, *The Christian Science Monitor*, June 10, 2013. http://www.csmonitor.com/World/Europe/2013/0610/UK-did-not-use-PRISM-to-dodge-British-law-says-Hague

56. "What the NSA's Massive Org Chart (Probably) Looks Like," by Marc Ambinder, Defense One, August 14, 2013. http://www.defenseone.com/ideas/2013/08/what-nsas-massive-org-chart-probably-looks/68642

57. "Who Holds Security Clearances?" *The Washington Post*, June 10, 2013. http://www.washingtonpost.com/world/who-holds-security-clearances/2013/06/10/983744e4-d232-11e2-a73e-826d299ff459_graphic.html

60. Statement by the President, June 7, 2013. https://www.whitehouse.gov/the-press-office/2013/06/07/statement-president

61. "Everything You Need to Know About PRISM," by T.C. Sottek and Joshua Kopstein, The Verge, July 17, 2013. http://www.theverge.com/2013/7/17/4517480/nsa-spying-prism-surveillance-cheat-sheet

62. "Did Edward Snowden Break His Oath?" by Amy Davidson, The New Yorker, January 5, 2014. http://www.newyorker.com/news/amy-davidson/did-edward-snowden-break-his-oath

68. "Birth of a Whistle-blower: How Edward Snowden Became Edward Snowden," by Luke Harding, Salon, February 7, 2014. http://www.salon.com/2014/02/07/birth_of_a_whistle_blower_how_edward_snowden_became_edward_snowden/

"NSA Leaker Was Shy, Computer-Bound Teenager in Maryland," by Julie Bykowicz and Greg Giroux, Bloomberg Business, June 11, 2013. http://www.bloomberg.com/news/articles/2013-06-11/nsa-leaker-was-shy-computer-bound-teenager-in-maryland

"Tracking Edward Snowden, from a Maryland Classroom to a Hong Kong Hotel," by Carol D. Leonnig, Jenna Johnson, and Marc Fisher, The Washington Post, June 15, 2013. http://www.washingtonpost.com/world/national-security/tracking-edward-snowden-from-a-maryland-classroom-to-a-hong-kong-hotel/2013/06/15/420aedd8-d44d-11e2-b05f-3ea3f0e7bb5a_story.html

"Former Neighbor Remembers Snowden as 'Nice Kid,'" by Greg Toppo, USA Today, June 10, 2013. http://www.usatoday.com/story/news/nation/2013/06/10/snowden-neighbors-surveillance-security/2408573/

69. "Details about Edward Snowden's Life in Maryland Emerge," by Jean Marbella, Shashank Bengali and David S. Cloud, The Baltimore Sun, June 10, 2013. http://articles.baltimoresun.com/2013-06-10/news/bs-md-snowden-profile-20130610_1_anne-arundel-county-arundel-high-the-guardian

71. "Tracking Edward Snowden, from a Maryland Classroom to a Hong Kong Hotel," by Carol D. Leonnig, Jenna Johnson, and Marc Fisher.

72. Ibid.

74. Ibid.

75. "Edward Snowden's Background Surrounded by Spycraft," by Adam Geller and Brian Witte, Associated Press, http://www.huffingtonpost.com/2013/06/15/edward-snowden-background_n_3446904.html

76. "NSA Is Looking for a Few Good Hackers," by Tabassum Zakaria, The Washington Post, August 2, 2011. http://www.washingtonpost.com/politics/nsa-is-looking-for-a-few-good-hackers/2011/08/02/gIQAXZAbqI_story.html

77. "Tracking Edward Snowden, from a Maryland Classroom to a Hong Kong Hotel," by Carol D. Leonnig, Jenna Johnson, and Marc Fisher.

78. "Everywhere in the world, every day, people's phone calls, emails and faxes are monitored by Echelon, a secret government surveillance network. No, it's not fiction straight out of George Orwell's 1984. It's reality, says former spy Mike Frost." From "Ex-Snoop Confirms Echelon Network," CBS News 60 Minutes, February 24, 2000. http://www.cbsnews.com/news/ex-snoop-confirms-echelon-network/

81. "Tracking Edward Snowden, from a Maryland Classroom to a Hong Kong Hotel," by Carol D. Leonnig, Jenna Johnson, and Marc Fisher.

82. "The Most Wanted Man in the World," by James Bamford, Wired, August 13, 2014. http://www.wired.com/2014/08/edward-snowden/

83. "Effort to Get NSA Leaker Edward Snowden's Father to Moscow Collapses," by Jerry Markon, The Washington Post, July 30, 2013. http://www.washingtonpost.com/politics/effort-to-get-nsa-leaker-edward-snowdens-father-to-moscow-collapses/2013/07/30/23e8875e-f949-11e2-b018-5b8251f0c56e_story.html

84. "Snowden as a Teen Online: Anime and Cheeky Humor," by Kristina Cooke and John Shiffman, Reuters, June 12, 2013. http://www.reuters.com/article/2013/06/12/us-usa-security-snowden-anime-idUSBRE95B14B20130612

86. "FBI Visits Family of NSA Leaker in Upper Macungie," by Colby Itkowitz and Daniel Patrick Sheehan, The Morning Call (Allentown, Pennsylvania), June 10, 2013. http://articles.mcall.

com/2013-06-10/news/mc-pa-ed-snowden-nsa-leak-20130610_1_fbi-agents-upper-macur-gie-township-public-records

87. "Children who have gone through a divorce, no matter what their age, can have difficulty with trust. They have felt betrayed by the people with whom they had the closest ties. These parent-child relationships are the models upon which future commitments are made, and are therefore an unsteady platform upon which to venture into romance and the attendant intimacy and trust." From *Difficult Questions Kids Ask and Are Afraid to Ask About Divorce*, by Meg F. Schneider and Joan Zuckerberg, page 197, Simon & Schuster, 1996.

88. "How Edward Snowden Went from Loyal NSA Contractor to Whistleblower," by Luke Harding, *The Guardian*, February 1, 2014. http://www.theguardian.com/world/2014/feb/01/edward-snowden-intelligence-leak-nsa-contractor-extract

89. "NSA Leaker Ed Snowden's Life on *Ars Technica*," by Joe Mullin, *Ars Technica*, June 12, 2013. http://arstechnica.com/tech-policy/2013/06/nsa-leaker-ed-snowdens-life-on-ars-technica/

Snowden's attorney Ben Wizner says his client "has never confirmed that he wrote these posts. He has said that people should be careful about attributing identities to anonymous online posts. The whole point of such forums is to allow people to try out new identities." However, Snowden hasn't denied that he was "The True HOOHA."

90. Ibid.

91. Ibid.

92. "Records Show Army Discharged Edward Snowden after 5 Months," by Stephanie Gaskell, *Politico*, June 10, 2013. http://www.politico.com/story/2013/06/edward-snowden-army-discharge-92486.html

93. "How Edward Snowden Went from Loyal NSA Contractor to Whistleblower," by Luke Harding.

94. "Snowden's Army Record: Short," by Tom Vanden Brook, *USA Today*, June 10, 2013. http://www.usatoday.com/story/news/nation/2013/06/10/snowdens-army-career-lasted-only-five-months/2407855/

95. "Ex-Worker at C.I.A. Says He Leaked Data on Surveillance," by Mark Mazzetti and Michael S. Schmidt, *The New York Times*, June 9, 2013. http://www.nytimes.com/2013/06/10/us/former-cia-worker-says-he-leaked-surveillance-data.html

96. "I Would Have Hired Edward Snowden," by David Auerbach, *Slate*, June 18, 2013. http://www.slate.com/articles/technology/technology/2013/06/i_would_have_hired_nsa_whistleblower_edward_snowden.html

For a good overview of the views of those who believe his story is too good to be true, see "Here Come the Edward Snowden Truthers," by Alex Seitz-Wald, *Salon*, June 19, 2013. http://www.salon.com/2013/06/19/here_come_the_edward_snowden_truthers/

97. "Investigators Looking at How Snowden Gained Access at NSA," by Peter Finn, Greg Miller, and Ellen Nakashima, *The Washington Post*, June 10, 2013. http://www.washingtonpost.com/world/national-security/investigators-looking-at-how-snowden-gained-access-at-nsa/2013/06/10/83b4841a-d209-11e2-8cbe-1bcbee06f8f8_story.html

"The research done at CASL ranges from cultural and linguistic studies to work on 'spycraft' technology. One neuroscience project reportedly focused on filling in the blanks of incomplete texts, such as documents from corrupted hard drives or intercepted communications … The university administration has touted its NSA partnership." From "What Happens in the University of Maryland NSA Facility Where Edward Snowden Worked?" by Asawin Suebsaeng, *Mother Jones*, June 12, 2013. http://www.motherjones.com/mojo/2013/06/university-maryland-edward-snowden-nsa

98. "C.I.A. Disputes Early Suspicions on Snowden," by Eric Schmitt, *The New York Times*, October 11, 2013. http://www.nytimes.com/2013/10/12/us/cia-disputes-early-suspicions-on-snowden.html

99. "Edward Snowden Reveals Himself as NSA Whistleblower," by Kim Zetter, *Wired*, June 10, 2013. http://www.wired.co.uk/news/archive/2013-06/10/edward-snowden

100. "Birth of a Whistle-blower: How Edward Snowden Became Edward Snowden," by Luke Harding.

104. "NSA Leaker Edward Snowden: Spy, Patriot, Libertarian, Communist, or What? The Man Washington Can't Figure Out," by Pema Levy, *International Business Times*, June 28, 2013. http://www.

ibtimes.com/nsa-leaker-edward-snowden-spy-patriot-libertarian-communist-or-what-man-washington-cant-figure-out

105. Snowden was reacting to Obama's appointment of Leon Panetta, who had previously served as president Bill Clinton's chief of staff, as director of National Intelligence. "Would You Feel Differently about Snowden, Greenwald, and Assange If You Knew What They Really Thought?" by Sean Wilentz, *The New Republic*, January 19, 2014. http://www.newrepublic.com/article/116253/edward-snowden-glenn-greenwald-julian-assange-what-they-believe

106. "Swiss to Press U.S. Further on Snowden's Time in Geneva," by Tom Miles, Reuters, June 27, 2013. http://www.reuters.com/article/2013/06/27/us-usa-security-snowden-switzerland-idUS-BRE95Q0RV20130627. Swiss officials have denied Snowden's story.

107. "Bush and Obama Spurred Edward Snowden to Spill U.S. Secrets," by Conor Friedersdorf, *The Atlantic*, August 22, 2014. http://www.theatlantic.com/politics/archive/2014/08/the-misdeeds-that-prompted-edward-snowden-to-spill-us-secrets/378963/

108. "How Edward Snowden Went from Loyal NSA Contractor to Whistleblower," by Luke Harding.

109. "The Snowden Saga: A Shadowland of Secrets and Light," by Bryan Burrough, Sarah Ellison, and Suzanna Andrews, *Vanity Fair*, May 2014. http://www.vanityfair.com/news/politics/2014/05/edward-snowden-politics-interview

110. "Snowden Says He Took No Secret Files to Russia," by James Risen, *The New York Times*, October 17, 2013. http://www.nytimes.com/2013/10/18/world/snowden-says-he-took-no-secret-files-to-russia.html

111. "Chatting about Japan with Snowden, the NSA Whistle-blower," by Christopher Johnson, *The Japan Times*, June 18, 2013. http://www.japantimes.co.jp/community/2013/06/18/issues/chatting-about-japan-with-snowden-the-nsa-whistle-blower

112. "The Most Wanted Man in the World," by James Bamford.

114. "Four Years Ago, Ed Snowden Thought Leakers Should Be 'Shot,'" by Timothy B. Lee, *The Washington Post*, June 26, 2013. http://www.washingtonpost.com/blogs/wonkblog/wp/2013/06/26/four-years-ago-ed-snowden-thought-leakers-should-be-shot/

115. "Edward Snowden: The Whistleblower Behind the NSA Surveillance Revelations," by Glenn Greenwald, Ewen MacAskill, and Laura Poitras, *The Guardian*, June 11, 2013. http://www.theguardian.com/world/2013/jun/09/edward-snowden-nsa-whistleblower-surveillance

116. "How Edward Snowden Went from Loyal NSA Contractor to Whistleblower," by Luke Harding.

119. U.S. Department of Labor website: http://www.whistleblowers.gov/
"Pentagon Papers Leaker: 'I was Bradley Manning,'" by Ashley Fantz, CNN, March 21, 2011. http://www.cnn.com/2011/US/03/19/wikileaks.ellsberg.manning/

120. For example, "Date-night for a Traitor: NSA Whistleblower Edward Snowden Enjoys Trip to the Theatre with Pole Dancer Girlfriend—as Lawyer Hints the Pair May Soon Marry in Moscow," by Will Stewart, *The Daily Mail*, October 14, 2014. http://www.dailymail.co.uk/news/article-2792940/ed-snowden-enjoys-date-theatre-pole-dancer-girlfriend-lawyer-hints-pair-soon-marry-moscow.html
The quotes come from, respectively, columnist Richard Cohen of *The Washington Post* and Bob Schieffer on CBS' *Face the Nation*. "The Snowden Psychiatric Smear," by Emily Masters, FAIR.org, August 1, 2013.

121. "[The Manning verdict and sentence] signals pretty clearly that if the U.S. ever gets its hands on Snowden—still encamped in the transit lounge of Sheremetyevo Airport in Moscow—he can expect no mercy. In his case, that would be not just another example of prosecutorial overkill, but just possibly a missed opportunity." From "Manning and Snowden," by Bill Keller, *The New York Times*, July 30, 2013. http://keller.blogs.nytimes.com/2013/07/30/manning-and-snowden

122. "Many in Media Claim Bradley Manning's Leaks Had Little Value—Here's Why They're So Wrong," by Greg Mitchell, *The Nation*, June 13, 2013. http://www.thenation.com/blog/174795/many-media-claim-bradley-mannings-leaks-had-little-value-heres-why-theyre-so-wrong

123. "Wikileaker Bradley Manning Awarded 112-Day Prison Credit for Military's Abuse," by Kim Zetter, *Wired*, January 8, 2013. http://www.wired.com/2013/01/manning-gets-sentencing-credit/

"Bradley Manning Sentenced to 35 Years in WikiLeaks Case," by Julie Tate, *The Washington Post*, August 21, 2013. http://www.washingtonpost.com/world/national-security/judge-to-sentence-bradley-manning-today/2013/08/20/85bee184-09d0-11e3-b87c-476db8ac34cd_story.html

124. "Before Snowden: The Whistleblowers Who Tried to Lift the Veil," by David Welna, NPR, July 22, 2014. http://www.npr.org/2014/07/22/333741495/before-snowden-the-whistleblowers-who-tried-to-lift-the-veil

125-135. Personal interview with Thomas Drake.

129. "The Secret Sharer," by Jane Mayer, *The New Yorker*, May 23, 2011. http://www.newyorker.com/magazine/2011/05/23/the-secret-sharer

136. "Loopholes Exclude Intelligence Contractors Like Snowden from Whistleblower Protections," by Pema Levy, *International Business Times*, July 11, 2013. http://www.ibtimes.com/loopholes-exclude-intelligence-contractors-snowden-whistleblower-protections-1301913

"N.S.A. Latest: The Secret History of Domestic Surveillance," by John Cassidy, *The New Yorker*, June 27, 2013. http://www.newyorker.com/news/john-cassidy/n-s-a-latest-the-secret-history-of-domestic-surveillance

137. "Contractor Fires Snowden from $122,000-a-year Job," by John Bacon, *USA Today*, June 11, 2013. http://www.usatoday.com/story/news/nation/2013/06/11/booz-allen-snowden-fired/2411231/

"Feds Hunted for Snowden in Days Before NSA Programs Went Public," by Mark Hosenball, Reuters, June 12, 2013. http://www.reuters.com/article/2013/06/12/us-usa-security-snowden-hunt-idUSBRE95B1A220130612

138. "Snowden Smuggled Documents from NSA on a Thumb Drive," by Kim Zetter, *Wired*, June 13, 2013. http://www.wired.com/2013/06/snowden-thumb-drive/

"On This Day Last Year, Snowden Took 4 'Empty' Laptops to Hong Kong—Here's Why," by Michael B. Kelley, *Business Insider*, May 20, 2014. http://www.businessinsider.com/why-snowden-had-4-laptops-to-hong-kong-2014-5

139. "How Edward Snowden Stole his Cache of NSA Secrets," by Peter Weber, The Week, June 14, 2013. http://theweek.com/articles/463185/how-edward-snowden-stole-cache-nsa-secrets

"What We Know About NSA Leaker Edward Snowden," NBC News, June 10, 2013. http://usnews.nbcnews.com/_news/2013/06/10/18882615-what-we-know-about-nsa-leaker-edward-snowden

140. "How Laura Poitras Helped Snowden Spill His Secrets," by Peter Maass, *The New York Times*, August 13, 2013. http://www.nytimes.com/2013/08/18/magazine/laura-poitras-snowden.html

144. "NSA Slides Explain the PRISM Data-collection Program," *The Washington Post*, July 10, 2013. http://www.washingtonpost.com/wp-srv/special/politics/prism-collection-documents

147. "Cheney Defends NSA, Calls Snowden a 'Traitor,'" Fox News, June 16, 2013. http://nation.foxnews.com/2013/06/16/cheney-defends-nsa-calls-snowden-traitor

"Hillary Clinton: Can 'Never Condone' What Edward Snowden Did," by David Sherfinski, *The Washington Times*, February 25, 2015. http://www.washingtontimes.com/news/2015/feb/25/hillary-clinton-can-never-condone-what-edward-snow/

148. "Edward Snowden, the N.S.A. Leaker, Comes Forward," by Amy Davidson, *The New Yorker*, June 9, 2013. http://www.newyorker.com/news/amy-davidson/edward-snowden-the-n-s-a-leaker-comes-forward

149. "True—he signed an executive order in October of 2012 that protects intelligence community whistleblowers. The Intelligence community is exempted from other whistleblower protections he signed into law in 2012. But that protection does not appear to do much for someone like Snowden, who wanted to blow the whistle to public on a classified program." From "Fact-checking Obama's Claims about Snowden," by Z. Byron Wolf, CNN, August 13, 2013. http://www.cnn.com/2013/08/12/politics/obama-snowden-whistleblower/

150. Snowden faces espionage charges in federal courts. "Unlike most of the state courts . . . the federal courts generally do not permit television or radio coverage of trial court proceedings." From the U.S. Federal Courts website: http://www.uscourts.gov/FederalCourts/UnderstandingtheFederalCourts/FederalCourtsAndThePublic.aspx

153. "Hasty Exit Started with Pizza Inside a Hong Kong Hideout," by Keith Bradsher, *The New York Times*, June 24, 2013. http://www.nytimes.com/2013/06/25/world/asia/snowden-departure-from-hong-kong.html

154. "Obama Administration Charges NSA Whistleblower Snowden with Espionage," RT, June 23, 2013. http://rt.com/usa/snowden-charged-espionage-sealed-092/

    "Edward Snowden's Departure from Hong Kong Filled with Intrigue, Questions," by Jia Lynn Yang, *The Washington Post*, June 24, 2013. http://www.washingtonpost.com/world/asia_pacific/edward-snowdens-departure-from-hong-kong-filled-with-intrigue-questions/2013/06/24/631d3a1a-dcc4-11e2-9218-bc2ac7cd44e2_story.html

155. Previously published media accounts of Snowden's departure from Hong Kong implied that Chinese officials let him board his flight to Russia despite the cancellation of his U.S. passport. See: "Russian media report: How Snowden Missed his Flight to Cuba," by Fred Weir, *The Christian Science Monitor*, August 26, 2013. http://www.csmonitor.com/World/Global-News/2013/0826/Russian-media-report-How-Snowden-missed-his-flight-to-Cuba. According to Ben Wizner, however, the cancellation notice went out after Snowden's departure.

156. "Ecuador Says Letter of Safe Conduct for Snowden is Real, but Unauthorized and Invalid," by Associated Press via Fox News, June 27, 2013. http://www.foxnews.com/world/2013/06/27/ecuador-says-letter-safe-conduct-for-snowden-is-real-but-unauthorized-and/

    According to Snowden's lawyer Ben Wizner, "Edward Snowden's passport was not canceled until he was up in the air, en route to Ecuador (via Moscow and Havana)."

158. "NSA Chief Keith Alexander: 'System Did Not Work As It Should Have' to Prevent Snowden Document Leaks," by Imtiyaz Delawala, ABC News, June 23, 2013. http://abcnews.go.com/blogs/politics/2013/06/nsa-chief-keith-alexander-system-did-not-work-as-it-should-have-to-prevent-snowden-document-leaks/

    "Sen. Feinstein Calls Snowden's NSA Leaks an 'Act of Treason,'" by Jeremy Herb and Justin Sink, The Hill, June 10, 2013. http://thehill.com/policy/defense/304573-sen-feinstein-snowdens-leaks-are-treason

159. "Boehner: Snowden is 'a Traitor,'" by Aaron Blake, *The Washington Post*, June 11, 2013. http://www.washingtonpost.com/blogs/post-politics/wp/2013/06/11/boehner-snowden-is-a-traitor/

    "Hillary Clinton: What Snowden Did 'Gave All Kinds of Information' to Terrorists," by Josh Feldman, *The Washington Post*, April 25, 2014. http://www.mediaite.com/online/hillary-clinton-what-snowden-did-gave-all-kinds-of-information-to-terrorists/

160. "Rand Paul 'Reserving Judgment' on Edward Snowden," by Ed O'Keefe, *The Washington Post*, June 11, 2013. http://www.washingtonpost.com/blogs/post-politics/wp/2013/06/11/rand-paul-reserving-judgment-on-edward-snowden/

    "Edward Snowden is Both a Patriot and a Traitor," by Michael B. Kelley, *Business Insider*, June 25, 2013. http://www.businessinsider.com/everybody-is-right-about-edward-snowden-2013-6#ixzz3YhvhcQlm

161. "GOP Congressman: Edward Snowden 'Defies Logic,' and the U.S. Should Do Everything It Can to Bring Him Back," by Brett Logiurato, *Business Insider*, June 23, 2013. http://www.businessinsider.com/mike-rogers-edward-snowden-nsa-russia-moscow-extradition-2013-6

163. "Snowden Says He Took No Secret Files to Russia," by James Risen.

164. "The Third Man on Snowden's Reading List," by Robert Mackey, *The New York Times*, July 24, 2013. http://thelede.blogs.nytimes.com/2013/07/24/the-third-man-on-snowdens-reading-list/

165. Snowden attorney Ben Wizner says his client was kept in a quarantine hotel, not the airport Novotel as had been widely reported.

    "Edward Snowden Has Not Entered Russia—Sergei Lavrov," by Jonathan Marcus, BBC, June 25, 2013. http://www.bbc.com/news/world-europe-23045790

166. "Joe Biden Asks Ecuador President Rafael Correa to Nix Edward Snowden Asylum," The Associated Press via *Politico*, June 30, 2013. http://www.politico.com/story/2013/06/edward-snowden-biden-ecuador-93594.html#ixzz3YhxpJhJu

167. "Obama on Snowden: 'I'm Not Going to be Scrambling Jets to Get a 29-year-old Hacker,'" by Dave Boyer, *The Washington Times*, June 27, 2013. http://www.washingtontimes.com/news/2013/jun/27/obama-snowden-im-not-going-be-scrambling-jets-get-/#ixzz3YhyEMThG

168. "Bolivian President's Plane Forced to Land in Austria in Hunt for Snowden," by Kathy Lally and Juan Forero, *The Washington Post*, July 3, 2013. http://www.washingtonpost.com/world/bolivian-presidents-plane-forced-to-land-in-austria-in-hunt-for-snowden/2013/07/03/c281c2f4-e3eb-11e2-a11e-c2ea876a8f30_story.html

169. "How a Snowdenista Kept the NSA Leaker Hidden in a Moscow Airport," by Sara Corbett, *Vogue*, February 19, 2015. http://www.vogue.com/11122973/sarah-harrison-edward-snowden-wikileaks-nsa/

170. "Snowden's New Talking Point: Nazi War Crimes Trial," by Michael Crowley, *Time*, July 13, 2013. http://swampland.time.com/2013/07/13/edward-snowden-invokes-historic-nazi-trial/

171. "Snowden Hopes for Temporary Asylum In Russia," by Mark Memmott, NPR, July 12, 2013. http://www.npr.org/blogs/thetwo-way/2013/07/12/201399605/snowden-to-meet-with-activists-issue-new-statement

172. "Statement by Edward Snowden to Human Rights Groups at Moscow's Sheremetyevo Airport," WikiLeaks, July 12, 2013. https://wikileaks.org/Statement-by-Edward-Snowden-to.html

173. Ibid.

174. "The Lost Language of Privacy," by David Brooks, *The New York Times*, April 14, 2015. http://www.nytimes.com/2015/04/14/opinion/david-brooks-the-lost-language-of-privacy.html

177. "Girlfriend Snowden 'Left' Lives with Him in Moscow," by Kate Briquelet, *The New York Post*, October 11, 2014. http://nypost.com/2014/10/11/snowdens-girlfriend-lives-with-him-in-moscow-documentary-reveals/

178. "Edward Snowden Gets Website Job in Russia, Lawyer Says," by Alla Eshchenko, CNN, October 31, 2013. http://www.cnn.com/2013/10/31/world/europe/russia-snowden-job/

179. "Edward Snowden: There's 'No Fair Trial Available' If I Return to the U.S.," Reuters via *The Huffington Post*, March 4, 2015. http://www.huffingtonpost.com/2015/03/04/edward-snowden-trial-us_n_6801506.html

185. "Claim on "Attacks Thwarted" by NSA Spreads Despite Lack of Evidence," by Justin Elliott and Theodoric Meyer, *ProPublica*, October 23, 2013. http://www.propublica.org/article/claim-on-attacks-thwarted-by-nsa-spreads-despite-lack-of-evidence

196. Congressman Jim Sensenbrenner's website about the USA Freedom Act: http://sensenbrenner.house.gov/legislation/theusafreedomact.htm

198. "The Quest to Build an NSA-Proof Cloud," by Michael Scaturro, *The Atlantic*, November 21, 2013. http://www.theatlantic.com/international/archive/2013/11/the-quest-to-build-an-nsa-proof-cloud/281704/

200. "FBI Director Attacks Tech Companies for Embracing New Modes of Encryption," by Spencer Ackerman, *The Guardian*, October 16, 2014. http://www.theguardian.com/us-news/2014/oct/16/fbi-director-attacks-tech-companies-encryption

201. "Parks Advocates Demand NYPD Returns Edward Snowden Statue Removed from Brooklyn Park," CBS New York, April 14, 2015. http://newyork.cbslocal.com/2015/04/14/parks-advocates-demand-nypd-returns-edward-snowden-statue-removed-from-brooklyn-park/

204. "Declassified Report Shows Doubts about Value of N.S.A.'s Warrantless Spying," by Charlie Savage, *The New York Times*, April 24, 2015. http://www.nytimes.com/2015/04/25/us/politics/value-of-nsa-warrantless-spying-is-doubted-in-declassified-reports.html

205. "Public Perceptions of Privacy and Security in the Post-Snowden Era," by Mary Madden, Pew Research Center, November 12, 2014. http://www.pewinternet.org/2014/11/12/public-privacy-perceptions/

207. "To Help Spread its Message, the NSA Has Produced a Coloring Book. You Know, for Kids," by Dan Raile, *Pando Daily*, April 25, 2015. http://pando.com/2015/04/25/to-help-spread-its-message-the-nsa-has-produced-a-coloring-book-you-know-for-kids/

208. "Spying is Cool? CryptoKids Appeal to Children in NSA Coloring Book," RT, April 27, 2015. http://rt.com/usa/253497-nsa-cryptokids-coloring-book/

209. "Edward Snowden Interviewed on *Last Week Tonight with John Oliver*," by Aditya Tejas, *International Business Times*, April 6, 2015. http://www.ibtimes.com/edward-snowden-interviewed-last-week-tonight-john-oliver-1870262

210. *Last Week Tonight with John Oliver*, "Government Surveillance," HBO, April 5, 2015. Video: https://www.youtube.com/watch?v=XEVlyP4_11M

About the Author

Cartoonist, journalist and graphic novelist Ted Rall is the editorial cartoonist for *The Los Angeles Times* and ANewDomain. net, a columnist for Creators Syndicate, and the author of numerous books of comics and prose journalism and commentary. His recent books include *After We Kill You, We Will Welcome You Back as Honored Guests: Unembedded in Afghanistan* and *The Book of Obama: From Hope and Change to the Age of Revolt*.

In 2007, *The New York Times* reported that Ted had come under surveillance by the New York Police Department.